A Tale of Two Kitchens

Mothers, Meals and Memories

A Tale of Two Kitchens

Mothers, Meals and Memories

LATA GWALANI

AMARYLLIS

AMARYLLIS

An imprint of Manjul Publishing House Pvt. Ltd.
• C-16, Sector 3, Noida, Uttar Pradesh 201 301, India
Website: www.manjulindia.com
Registered Office:
• 2nd Floor, Usha Preet Complex, 42 Malviya Nagar,
Bhopal 462 003 – India
Distribution Centres
Ahmedabad, Bengaluru, Chennai, Hyderabad,
Kochi, Kolkata, Mumbai, Noida, Pune

A Tale of Two Kitchens: Mothers, Meals and Memories by Lata Gwalani

This paperback edition first published in India in 2026

ISBN: 978-93-7317-367-2

Cover design: Neelima P Aryan

Photography: Nikhil Bendre
Illustrations: Anitha Rajagopal

Printed and bound in India by Nutech Print Services Pvt. Ltd.

Contents

Introduction

In two households where the aroma of curry leaves mingled with the gleaming hue of pureed tomatoes, a Tamilian mother and a Sindhi mother embarked on a journey that transcended the boundaries of language, culture, and geography. It began with an exchange of recipes, a casual sharing of spices and techniques, but eventually blossomed into a profound friendship forged over simmering pots and sizzling pans.

This memoir is more than a collection of recipes; it's a tapestry of life woven together with love, resilience, and the magic of food. From the tangy tamarind *rasam* that warms the soul, to the rich and hearty Sindhi *kadhi* that soothes the spirit, every dish here carries with it not just the flavours of two distinct culinary heritages but also the emotions, laughter, and wisdom of two remarkable women.

As their daughter and daughter-in-law, I have had the unparalleled privilege of standing at the crossroads of their culinary legacies. Over the years, I became not just a witness but a participant in their exchange—absorbing their lessons, embracing their techniques, and melding their traditions with touches of my own. My kitchen, today, is a tribute to their enduring bond, and their shared passion for cooking. It boasts a harmonious blend of their styles, where Tamilian delicacies meet Sindhi flavours, creating dishes that are as unique as the love story of these two women.

Every recipe in this book is more than just a set of instructions—it is a chapter of my life, steeped in memory and meaning. It is the story of how food can unite, heal, and celebrate. The sizzle of *rai* in hot oil and the rich aroma of slow-cooked *dal* are reminders of their wisdom, their strength, and their unconditional love.

This memoir is an invitation to step into a world where food is more than sustenance—it is a bridge between cultures, generations, cuisines, a language of love, and a celebration of identity. Let this book take you on a journey where culinary traditions come alive and kitchens become sanctuaries of shared dreams and enduring bonds.

A celebration of two mothers, their heritage, and the flavours that bring us together.

Food as a Leveller

Food has a way of bringing people together like nothing else. I've witnessed it first-hand. One of the most beautiful aspects of my marriage—me, a Tamilian, and my husband, a Sindhi—is how our two distinct cuisines intertwined early on. Ironically, it wasn't shared food that united our families; instead, it was the striking contrasts. The differences were what ignited conversations, especially between our mothers. While they exchanged recipes and marvelled at how different each was, we sat down to meals that were as much about discovery as they were about flavour.

Of course, it wasn't always smooth sailing. There were the occasional awkward moments, particularly when one of the mothers made an offhand remark that wasn't the easiest to digest. But then, Amma would bring out her aromatic, piping-hot rasam in a gleaming stainless steel *kinnam* (serving bowl) and Mamma would follow with her dainty china bowl, brimming with sizzling *aloo tikkis.* Those simple yet powerful exchanges were the glue that bound us and any minor grievances were forgiven, sometimes forgotten.

Amma and Mamma—two women from completely different worlds—came together over food.

The Two Mothers

Amma—the embodiment of the traditional Tamilian woman, from an Iyer family steeped in values, rituals, and an eternal supply of curd.

Mamma—my mother-in-law, a lively Sindhi woman with a zest for life. For her, if food wasn't tangy, spicy, and cooked until the oil left the sides, it wasn't worth bringing to the table.

Through the pages that follow, you'll discover how these two vastly different culinary worlds merged, creating a delightful fusion of flavours and traditions. The recipes you'll find here may not be what you know or what you can easily find online. These are the exact renditions from Amma's and Mamma's kitchens, with stories woven in between—a tapestry of their unique personalities and lifestyles.

Mamma is nodding her approval from her heavenly home, no doubt. Amma, on the other hand, knows about the making of this book but forgets the moment I turn my back. Her tired memory is content to stay in the present, but every night, without fail, she sets curd. Touchwood!

Kitchen Favourites: The Battle of the Cookers

When I first entered my Sindhi home, I was taken aback by the sheer *pressure* of the situation. No, not the family drama, but the pressure cookers that seemed to occupy every nook and cranny of the kitchen. It was like the cookers had taken over. Among the various sizes, there was one that stole my heart—the 2-litre cooker. Cuteness aside, it turned out to be the most used one. The Sindhi kitchen, I learned, was all about pressure cooking—*bhajis* and everything else were cooked directly in the body of the cooker. A bit unconventional, but hey, it worked.

This was a far cry from my upbringing. In Amma's kitchen, the crown jewel was the massive 5-litre pressure cooker. It had its permanent spot on the platform, surrounded by three containers stacked neatly on a stand. The top two containers were designated for rice (yes, both of them), while the third held *tuvar/toor/arhar* dal (split pigeon pea gram), which found its way into sambar, rasam, and basically every other dish in the repertoire. If *kootu* (similar to a vegetable stew) made an appearance that day, you could bet your last rupee that the third container had chopped veggies and *chana* dal (split Bengal gram). Three dishes, one cooker—Amma's idea of multitasking.

But while Amma's kitchen was minimalist in terms of the number of cookers, every dish had its own specific vessel. The sambar had its dedicated 'sambar pot,' the *eeya chombu* (a special metal pot) was reserved for making that tangy rasam, and the *cheenchetti* (a traditional clay pot) had the all-important job of cooking stir-fried vegetable dishes like *upperi* or the *poriyal.* While Amma's cooker may have been the one-stop shop for many meals, every dish still had its rightful place in her kitchen kingdom.

Water with a slice of lemon was always floating at the bottom of the stand in Amma's cooker, as essentials to prevent blackening of the cooker body. No direct cooking in the body of the cooker was ever executed—it was all about layering, like a carefully orchestrated cooking symphony.

Then I met the *sipri*, also known as *degh* (large cooking pot or cauldron) in Mamma's kitchen—and boy, was I in for a surprise? Here, rice was never pressure cooked. Oh no. Rice was boiled in a sipri which had a belly that could rival a pot-bellied uncle. Most rice dishes—biryani, pulao, *tairi*—were made in these, and Mamma had sipris in all shapes and sizes. The designated sipri cabinet was thus, like a culinary wardrobe of wonders.

As I write this, I've given away most of the sipris—some of them were so old, they looked like they could use a good spa treatment. But don't worry, new ones are already on the way. The sipri legacy is alive and well.

Over the years, I managed to convince Mamma to let me pressure cook the rice occasionally, you know, to avoid the teaspoon of oil and salt that went into the water when cooked in a sipri. Mamma reluctantly agreed, but when guests were around? The rice was always, and I mean always—*sipri*-ed. Guests from my side of the family must have thought we had some sacred rice-making ritual going on. Little did they know, it was all about that special sipri touch.

When They Visited Each Other: The Recipe Exchange Chronicles

The social visits between my two mothers were like a recipe exchange programme, sprinkled with hilarious conversations and the occasional raised eyebrow. And the humble *palak* (or *keerai*)—that green wonder, spinach—was the unsuspecting star of their culinary collaboration.

It all started innocently enough. One day, Amma, ever the curious cook, couldn't resist probing into Mamma's kitchen secrets. With a twinkle in her eye, she ventured, 'Oho, Sindhi *sai bhaji*? Very famous, no?'

Mamma, with her no-nonsense kitchen style, ladled another scoop of the vibrant dish into Amma's already overflowing bowl. 'Yes,' she replied matter-of-factly.

Amma, took a spoonful, and out tumbled a string of questions that could rival a police interrogation. 'Chana dal?' she asked.

'Yes,' Mamma confirmed.

'No coconut?'

'No,' Mamma shot back, with a knowing smile.

By now, you must have picked up on the pattern: Amma and Mamma communicated in a series of monosyllabic exchanges, often loaded with confusion and cultural quirks. Amma spoke Hindi in Tamil, while Mamma threw in a little Sindhi flair into her Hindi, which Amma never seemed to notice. Over time, this linguistic collision resulted in a whole new dialect—a mixture of Hindi, Tamil and Sindhi that was uniquely theirs. Their humble contribution to the world of languages.

Amma, never one to back down, tried to make a comparison, 'Little, little like our keerai *molagootal*,' she offered, taking another spoonful of the sai bhaji with satisfaction.

And just like that, a pattern was born: every time Mamma made sai bhaji, a generous portion would be set aside for Amma. In return, Amma would send over keerai molagootal from her kitchen, with a side of nostalgia and love. Mamma, with all her confidence, adopted the name 'keeramolgu'—she was sure that was the right one—and grew rather fond of the dish.

And so, this strange and charming relationship blossomed. From temple visits in South India to foot massages on the sunny beaches of Pattaya, the two mothers bonded like the diverse veggies that go into the colourful, lip-smacking *avial*—each one adding its own distinct flavour, but all coming together in perfect harmony. You could say it was a match made in culinary heaven.

Sai Bhaji: A Hearty, Wholesome Veggie Stew

(Serves 3)

Ingredients

- A bunch of fresh spinach—cleaned, chopped, and washed (green goodness)
- ½ cup soaked and drained chana dal (soaked for 15 minutes)
- 1 large onion, chopped
- 1 large tomato, chopped
- 1 bhindi (okra), chopped
- ½ brinjal (eggplant), chopped
- 1 small potato, chopped
- 2 green chillies, chopped (for a mild kick)

Method

1. Heat 2 tablespoons of your favourite cooking oil in a pressure cooker. The sizzle starts here.
2. Drop in the chopped green chillies and onions. Sauté until the onions soften and turn golden.
3. Add in the chopped tomatoes and all the other veggies—okra, brinjal, and potato. Give them a good stir and let them sauté for 5 minutes, soaking in all the flavours.
4. Toss in the chopped spinach and soaked chana dal. Stir everything together for that perfect veggie blend.
5. Sprinkle in a pinch of turmeric, salt to taste, dhania (coriander) powder, jeera (cumin) powder and red chilli powder (optional, but why not add some heat if you like it spicy).
6. Add water to cover the veggies in the cooker—don't skimp on that essential veggie broth.
7. Stir well, close the lid of the cooker, and let it cook under pressure for 2 whistles.
8. After 10 minutes, switch off the gas and let the pressure cooker cool. Patience, patience.
9. Once cool, open the lid and—here comes the magic—whisk the contents into a smooth, creamy consistency. (You can use a blender but Mamma swore by the wooden whisk.)
10. Serve this comforting, green goodness hot with *bhuga chawal* (rice cooked with spices and browned with caramelised onions for that extra touch of flavour) or with plain steamed rice.

Pro Tip

This dish is packed with nutritious veggies, lentils and that comforting, earthy flavour. It's one of those dishes that just gets better the next day.

Keerai Molagootal: A Green, Hearty Delight

(Serves 3)

Ingredients

- A bunch of fresh spinach, cleaned, chopped, and washed
- ½ cup tuvar dal (cooked and mashed)
- 1 tbsp freshly grated coconut (because everything's better with coconut)
- ½ tsp cumin seeds
- Coconut oil for tempering (a splash of flavour)
- ¼ tsp rai (relatively smaller black-brown mustard seeds)
- ¼ tsp urad dal (split skinned black gram)
- 1 sprig of curry leaves
- 1–2 dried red chillies (add more if you're feeling adventurous)
- Salt, to taste
- A pinch of turmeric (for that golden glow)

Method

1. In a thick-bottomed vessel, add just enough water to cover the spinach. Bring it to a gentle boil.
2. Toss in a pinch of salt and turmeric, letting it simmer for about 5 minutes.
3. Drain the spinach and set it aside to cool. (Keep the water, it's full of goodness)
4. While the spinach cools, grind the coconut and cumin seeds into a smooth paste. Add a little water as needed. If you like it thicker, throw in a handful of washed raw rice for extra texture.
5. Pour this creamy coconut paste into a bowl and set it aside.
6. In the same grinder, quickly pulse the cooled spinach into a fine, smooth paste.
7. Now, take the spinach water (saved earlier) and bring it to a boil on high heat.
8. Stir in the spinach paste into the boiling water and add some salt for flavour.
9. Add the mashed tuvar dal and give everything a good, hearty mix.
10. When it starts bubbling, reduce the heat and add in the coconut paste.
11. Let the spinach froth and simmer gently, but don't let it come to a full boil. Patience, my friend.
12. Meanwhile, heat a little coconut oil in a skillet. Add rai, dried red chillies, urad dal and curry leaves.
13. When the rai starts spluttering and the aroma fills your kitchen, pour this glorious tempering over the simmering molagootal.
14. Switch off the gas, and let the flavours settle.
15. Serve with hot steamed rice, a dollop of ghee, crispy *appalam* (fried *papadam*) and a tangy lemon pickle.

Pro Tip

This dish is like a hug in a bowl—comforting, healthy and packed with flavour. The coconut gives it that creamy richness, while the tempering adds a sizzle of excitement.

Roots: Survival and Spice

Mamma's story is one of grit and grace. She hailed from a community of survivors who, after losing their lavish homes, started fresh from humble refugee camps. These resilient folks had built empires out of nothing, and the young girls, including my feisty Mamma, learned the sacred arts of embroidery, sewing and making pickles and papads. These skills didn't just help them to pass time—they became a golden ticket to financial stability. Money-making came first, education second. But here's the twist: the very immigrants who prioritised survival went on to establish some of the country's top educational institutions. Talk about a plot twist.

Amma, on the other hand, came from a totally different world. She grew up in a lavish household where heritage wasn't just something to admire from afar—it was a part of every corner of her life. The girls were groomed for marriage (yes, *that* kind of preparation), but they didn't stop at that. Amma went to an English-medium school, read Shakespeare like a pro, and even performed his plays. Classical music and Bharatanatyam were also on the agenda. Her childhood was a delicate balance of piety and perfection, where God was hailed with every step you took in her grand house. Seriously, you could probably turn a corner and bump into a deity.

Speaking of roots and resilience, let's talk about the lotus stem (also known as the lotus root), or *beeh*, which holds a special place in Sindhi and Tamilian kitchens alike. In Sindhi cuisine, beeh *basar* and beeh tikki are delicacies made from this wonderfully slimy (yet totally delicious) vegetable that grows in marshy, muddy waters. Back in the day, the stem would arrive home looking like it had been through a swamp adventure—so cleaning it thoroughly was an art of its own. Luckily, now we get partially cleaned stems. Meanwhile, the Tamilians have their own version, *tamarai kizhangu vathal*—a crispy treat that's a fry-up like no other. Two cultures, one root—and a whole lot of flavour.

Beeh Basar: A Comforting, Flavourful Delight

(Serves 3)

Ingredients

- 250 gm lotus stem, cleaned and sliced into thick diagonal pieces (don't worry if it's a little stringy—that's totally normal)
- 3–4 medium-sized onions, finely chopped
- 3–4 ripe tomatoes, finely chopped
- 1–2 medium-sized potatoes, peeled and diced
- 3–4 green chillies, finely chopped (spice lovers, rejoice)
- A sprig of fresh coriander (for that burst of freshness)
- 3–4 whole black peppercorns
- 1 tsp cumin seeds
- 1 tsp turmeric
- Red chilli powder, to taste (adjust as per your spice tolerance)
- Salt, to taste
- 1 tsp coriander powder
- 1 tsp cumin powder
- 1 tbsp cooking oil of choice

Method

1. Heat the cooking oil in a pressure cooker—this is where all the magic begins.
2. Drop in the cumin seeds and whole black peppercorns letting them sizzle and release their wonderful aroma.
3. Toss in the chopped green chillies and onions, sautéing them until the onions turn golden and fragrant.
4. Add the chopped tomatoes and a pinch of salt, stirring until the tomatoes break down into a mushy, flavourful paste.

5. Pour in a ladle of water to loosen up the mixture, then cover the cooker with its lid.
6. Let it whistle twice and turn off the stove.
7. Allow the pressure cooker to cool down before opening it up.
8. Once cool, give the onion-tomato mixture a good whisk until smooth and well-blended.

9. Turn the gas back on and add in the diced potatoes and sliced lotus stem.
10. Mix them well, making sure each piece is coated with the rich onion-tomato paste.
11. Sprinkle in the remaining salt, turmeric, red chilli powder, coriander powder and cumin powder. Give it all a good stir.
12. Add 2–3 ladles of water (or more if you prefer a soupy consistency). Let it all come to a gentle boil.
13. Cover the cooker again, and let it cook on medium flame for another 2 whistles.
14. Turn off the gas and wait for the cooker to cool down.
15. Garnish with freshly chopped coriander, adding that pop of green and freshness.
16. Serve with hot rice or soft chapatis and watch this delicious dish gulped down with gusto.

Pro Tip

This comforting dish pairs perfectly with any Indian flatbread or a bowl of fluffy rice. It's the perfect mix of heartiness, spice, and comfort.

The Legendary *Tamarai Kizhangu Vathal* Saga

Amma's trips to the local Tamil grocer in Mumbai were nothing short of an adventure. She'd waltz in and without fail, emerge victorious with a prized packet of tamarai kizhangu vathal. For the uninitiated, tamarai kizhangu is Tamil for lotus stem, and vathal? Well, that's the crispy fried goodness we all crave. These little gems are made by marinating diced lotus stem in a tantalising mix of salt, tamarind, chilli powder and turmeric, then sun-drying them until they're as crispy as a summer breeze. The end result? A packet of pure joy, ready to be deep-fried and served alongside rice—be it with sambar, rasam, or—my personal favourite—with *thayir sadam* (rice and curd). Oh, the flavour.

One afternoon, Amma proudly presented a plate of freshly fried tamarai vathal at lunch. The golden crunchiness was calling my name. But Mamma, ever the sceptic, raised an eyebrow at the vathal's dark (read: almost burnt) colour. After a moment's hesitation, though, she recognised—*asanjo* beeh (our beeh)—and took a cautious bite. And voilà! The crunchy, crispy vathal became an instant hit in our house. From wary to wow, that's the magic of food, isn't it?

Roots: Can Stems Be Far Behind?

Now, if we're talking roots, can stems really be far behind? In my Tamilian home, one humble hero that never failed to make an appearance was the banana tree stem. Enter: *vazhaithandu mor* kootu—a dish that's as wholesome as it sounds.

This glorious creation, a unique side dish, is one of those nostalgic recipes that sadly, has slipped through the cracks of my cooking routine. Not that I'm crying over spilled milk or in this case, over missed meals. But I'll be honest, I haven't made it in my kitchen for ages. I solemnly swear, though, that it will make a comeback soon.

Vazhaithandu mor kootu is the perfect pairing for a fiery, tangy *chinna vengaya* vatha *kuzhambu* (recipe follows on the heels of this one). Together, they create a delightful dance of flavours. I may have neglected this dish, but like the stem itself, it's time for it to rise again in my kitchen.

Vazhaithandu Mor Kootu: A Creamy, Cooling Delight

(Serves 3)

Ingredients

- 1 vazhaithandu (banana stem)
- ½ cup curd
- 5 green chillies (adjust to your spice level)
- 4 curry leaves
- Salt, to taste

For Tempering

- 2 tsp oil (or coconut oil for that extra flavour)
- ½ tsp rai
- 1 tsp urad dal
- 6 curry leaves

For Grinding

- ½ cup grated coconut
- ¾ tsp cumin seeds
- 4 green chillies
- 1 tsp rice flour (for that lovely, thick texture)

Method

1. Start by peeling the skin off the banana stem—you'll see it comes off in separate rings. Cut the stem into small thin cubes. Feel free to remove any fibre as you go.
2. Once cut, pop the cubes into a bowl of water with a dash of diluted curd to keep it fresh until you're ready to cook.
3. Grind the coconut, green chillies, cumin, and rice flour with a little water to make a smooth, creamy paste. (This is where the magic happens.)
4. Boil water in a pan and drain and drop in the banana stem cubes with a pinch of salt until tender.
5. Meanwhile, beat the curd well for a creamy consistency. Once the cubes are cooked, add in the coconut paste and give it a good mix. Bring to a gentle boil, then turn off the flame.
6. Add the beaten curd and stir gently.
7. Now, the fun part—temper it. Heat oil in a pan, add rai, urad dal and curry leaves. Let them crackle, then pour this fragrant tempering over your kootu and mix well.

Pro Tip

This dish is best served hot with rice, or as a side dish with any South Indian meal. The combination of curd, coconut, and banana stem is super refreshing and perfect for any season.

Chinna Vengaya Vatha Kuzhambu: Small Bomb, Big Burst of Flavour

There's something about the combination of small Madras onions cooked in a tangy, spicy tamarind gravy that makes this dish an absolute winner with hot, steaming rice. Whenever Amma ran out of vegetables, she whipped up this vatha kuzhambu. There was always a bunch of chinna *vengayam* (Madras onion) in the onion basket in Amma's kitchen. She would dunk them in water for a while so she could peel them easily.

This kuzhambu is perfect for quick fix cooking—no fuss, just flavour. And it became a hero in my Sindhi household. Best eaten the next day, when the spices and the tamarind reach the finest piquancy. Mamma, a fan of anything fiery and pungent, relished this either with rice or simply by itself.

(Serves 3)

Ingredients

- 1 large ball of tamarind
- 1 cup small onions, peeled and uncut
- 1½ tbsp sambar powder
- 1 tsp salt (adjust to taste)
- 1 tbsp rice flour

For Tempering

- 2 tbsp sesame oil
- 1 tsp rai
- ½ tsp methi (fenugreek seeds)
- ½ tsp ajwain (carom seeds)
- Some curry leaves
- A few dried red chillies

Method

1. Soak the tamarind in warm water for 10 minutes and extract the juice. Set aside.
2. In the meantime, heat sesame oil in a pan. Add rai and let them splutter. Then, add the fenugreek and carom seeds, the curry leaves, and the red chillies. Give it a quick mix.

3. Add the peeled onions and sauté until they turn translucent.
4. Stir in the sambar powder and cook until it turns a bit brown and aromatic.
5. Lower the heat, and then add the tamarind extract and salt. Let this simmer for 5 minutes.
6. While it's boiling, mix rice flour with just enough water to form a paste. Add this paste to the kuzhambu to thicken it. You can adjust the consistency by adding more water, as needed.
7. Let it boil for another few minutes and then switch off the heat.

Pro Tip

Amma always dropped in a small chunk of jaggery at this stage just to set the balance right.

Serve this lip-smacking vengaya vatha kuzhambu with hot rice, a drizzle of sesame oil and some pappadam on the side. And of course, with the vazhaithandu mor kootu. Enjoy the burst of flavours with every bite.

Dips and Sides: Spice It Up

If there's one dish in Tamilian cuisine that could rival the variety of gods on every temple altar, it's *thogayal*—that fiery, flavourful dip that comes in as many avatars as there are spices in Amma's kitchen. It's essentially a chutney, but trust me, it's so much more than that.

Amma's thogayal creations were always on point, mixing the perfect balance of spices, tang, and heat. The base recipe? Unchanging. But what made each batch stand out was the magic mix of veggies she tossed in. From the fiery vengaya thogayal (onion dip) to the tangy *thakkali* thogayal (green tomato dip) to the smoky *katharikkai* thogayal (brinjal dip), each one brought its own personality to the table. But the undisputed champion in our house? The *paruppu* thogayal (crumbled dal chutney). This wasn't just a dip; it was an earthy, nutty symphony that made every meal feel like a feast.

Paruppu Thogayal: Earthy and a Perfect Partner

(Serves 3)

Ingredients

- 1/4 cup tuvar dal
- 1/4 cup chana dal
- 1/2 tsp whole black pepper
- 4–5 dried red chillies
- 2 tbsp grated coconut (optional, but so worth it)
- A pinch of hing (asafoetida)

- 1 tsp oil
- Salt, to taste

Method

1. Heat up that teaspoon of oil in a pan and give the red chillies and asafoetida a quick, fragrant fry. Set them aside—they've earned a break.
2. In the same pan, toss in the tuvar dal, chana dal and whole black pepper. Sauté them on a medium flame until the dal turns a gorgeous golden brown (watch for that nutty aroma—it's divine).
3. Add the grated coconut to the mix and give it a quick sauté for 2–3 seconds. Then switch off the flame. (The coconut's work here is subtle but oh-so-important.)
4. Once the mixture cools, blend it with a splash of water and just enough salt. Aim for a coarse paste—it's all about texture.
5. Serve this delightful thogayal with steaming hot rice, a drizzle of ghee and watch it disappear faster than you can say 'seconds'.

Variations

- Feeling minimal? Skip the chana dal and use tuvar dal alone—it's just as fab.
- Garlic lover? Toss in 2 garlic cloves while frying the dal for an extra punch of flavour.
- Coconut is optional, but honestly, it's the unique selling point of this recipe.

Pair this thogayal magic with some comforting rasam and let your taste buds do a happy dance.

Zesty Green Chutney: The All-Rounder of Your Kitchen

While the Tamilian thogayal danced effortlessly between partners, adapting to any dish with ease, the green chutney of my Sindhi household stood firm in its resolve. Unyielding and steadfast, it has always been a constant presence at our meals—a quiet yet bold declaration of tradition. Even today, a gleaming stainless steel *dabba* (box)—the cherished chutney dabba—sits proudly in my fridge, always brimming with this zesty staple, ready to add its vibrant flavour to every plate.

(Fills a medium-sized dabba)

Ingredients

- A big bunch of fresh coriander, cleaned and chopped
- A smaller bunch of fresh mint, cleaned and chopped
- 2 medium-sized onions, roughly chopped into chunks
- 4–5 green chillies (or fewer if you're feeling mild today)
- 1 tsp cumin seeds
- Salt, to taste
- 1 juicy lemon

Method

1. Pop all the ingredients (except the lemon) into a blender and give it a whirl. Add a few drops of water to get that perfect, smooth consistency—thick enough to scoop, yet easy to spread.
2. Transfer this vibrant green magic into a bowl.
3. Squeeze in some fresh lemon juice for that tangy kick—adjust to your liking, of course.

Pro Tip

Store this flavourful goodness in an airtight steel dabba in the refrigerator. It'll happily hang out for up to a week, waiting to spice up your meals.

This chutney is the life of the party—pair it with parathas, cutlets, dosa, idli or slather it generously between bread slices for the ultimate chutney sandwich.

In my Sindhi household, this green chutney is a staple—a zesty companion that adds a burst of flavour to just about anything. Try it, and let your meals come alive with its bold, fresh taste.

Of Ribbons and Pakoras: Crispy Bites of Love and Laughter

The rain battered the windows; a symphony of thunder and splashes that made it seem like the sky was throwing a full-on tantrum. The wind joined in, howling through the partly open window like it had a personal vendetta against the warmth inside. It was only 4 p.m., but you'd swear it was 10 p.m. already—the kind of cozy twilight that makes you want to wrap yourself in a blanket and never leave the house. The lights in the house were already on, casting a warm glow to the surroundings.

Amma was visiting, and it was one of those magical afternoons when the house felt full of laughter, love, and the delightful hum of two generations chatting away in their version of Hindi. They had their own way of speaking—a special dialect only they understood. Their words flowed effortlessly, a blend of nostalgia and memories of childhood peppered with inside jokes only they could decode.

Mamma, always quick on her feet, rose from her comfy spot where they had been chatting for hours, and declared, 'Time for *pakoras*[1]!'

The Tamil version is pakoda and the Sindhi version is pakora.

'Ah, *sanna pakora*,' she added with a twinkle in her eye, like it was the most natural thing to say.

Amma blinked, clearly caught off guard. '*Ribbon pakoda?*' she asked, surprised by the sudden announcement.

Mamma shook her head, grinning. 'Ribbon? No,' she said, her voice firm but playful, like she had just discovered a culinary imposter in the middle of her kitchen.

I, sensing the impending clash of culinary cultures, quickly jumped in to save the day before it became a full-on wrestling match of words.

'No, no, ribbon pakoda is different from sanna pakora, Amma,' I explained, with my best 'I'm the voice of reason' tone. I could see the confusion in Mamma's eyes, but she was intrigued enough to settle back down on the sofa, waiting for me to untangle this mystery for her.

Amma, now fully invested in this impromptu cooking session, couldn't help but chuckle at the mix-up. 'I will tell you how to make ribbon pakoda,' she said, her enthusiasm growing by the second. 'It's all about the batter and the right amount of crispiness.'

The room felt warmer with each passing moment, not just from the explanation but from the energy between them. Mamma leaned forward, her curiosity piqued. It wasn't every day she got to witness Amma's recipe secrets.

And there we were, in the middle of a cozy rainy afternoon, with two generations of cooks about to share their wisdom and laughs over something as simple yet sacred, as pakoras. It was the kind of moment you didn't want to end, and it felt like the rain outside had slowed down just to listen in.

The ribbon pakoda is my absolute throwback to Deepavali—the one festival where everything smells like ghee and feels like home. A few days before the grand event, Amma would go into a full-

on festival preparation mode. Out came the *kuthu vilakku* (standing lamps), the *pithalai vilakku* (the brass ones) and she'd scrub them all down with salt and tamarind—because why not add a little extra sparkle to the festival of lights?

Now, let's talk about the crown jewel of Amma's kitchen during Deepavali: ribbon pakoda. Yeah, yeah, there were a ton of sweets and snacks being whipped up, but this crispy beauty was *the one*. And to be honest, it wasn't just the crispy, golden goodness that got me hooked—it was the name. Ribbon pakoda. Sounds fancy, right? Like it should come with a ribbon-tied bow and a royal entrance.

But there was something else that totally fascinated me: the mould.

Amma's pakoda-making game came with a serious tool—this common mould, decked out with all sorts of brass plates to make ribbons, *sev, murukku*... you name it. It was the kind of kitchen gadget that made me feel like I was about to join a gourmet chef's army—and no, it wasn't just a tool, it was a weapon.

The ribbons themselves? Well, they were more than just crunchy snacks—they were my entry ticket to the Deepavali magic. No wonder I was always so obsessed with them.

Ribbon Pakoda: Crispy, Spicy, Irresistible

(Serves 3)

Ingredients

- 2 cups of besan (Bengal gram flour)
- 2 cups rice flour (*for the crunch factor*)
- A pinch of asafoetida
- Chilli powder, as per taste (the more, the merrier)
- Butter, less than 50 gm butter (because even a little bit makes everything better)
- Salt, to taste

Method

1. Mix the besan and rice flour together in a bowl—get it nice and blended.
2. Add asafoetida, butter, salt, and chilli powder. Slowly add water, kneading it into a soft dough. (Hint: The dough shouldn't stick to your hands—if it does, add a little more flour.)
3. Once your dough is ready:
   - Heat the oil

- Stuff the dough into the mould and attach the ribbon pakoda plate to the bottom of the mould
- Press the dough into the oil in a circular motion
- Fry until golden brown and crispy

4. Once done, remove, drain, and repeat the frying magic until all the dough is gone.

Pro Tip

These pakodas are perfect as a crunchy snack, with tea or even as a side dish to spice up any meal.

Warning: They disappear fast!

Sanna Pakora: Crispy, Spicy Bites of Heaven

Let's talk about the *sanna pakora*, loosely known as Sindhi pakora. Now, don't be fooled by the simple name, because there's more to this snack than meets the eye. The sanna pakora (which means 'tiny' or 'small' in Sindhi) isn't your run-of-the-mill, one-fry wonder. Oh no, my friends, this little gem gets the VIP treatment: it's fried *twice*. And when I say twice, I mean *TWICE*. Because why settle for mediocre when you can have double the crunch, double the golden perfection?

Now, I know some of you out there might be raising an eyebrow, clutching your green smoothies, and side-eyeing these crispy beauties. Yes, it's a little indulgent. Yes, it's double-fried. But honestly, *your loss* if you don't indulge. Sometimes, you've got to throw that diet out the window and embrace the crispy, fried joy that is life. And hey, if you really need to convince yourself, think of it as 'flavour packed into two crispy layers of heaven.' Just saying.

But back to the sanna pakora. You've got this tiny, golden morsel of deliciousness, fried to perfection, and let me tell you—it's not just food, it's a whole experience. Every bite is a crunchy, savoury moment that takes you back to family gatherings, rainy afternoons or that one time you just *needed* something to lift your spirits. And if you really want to get technical, it's got that perfect ratio of soft interior to crispy exterior. It's got finesse, it's got flair and most importantly, it's got flavour.

So, the next time someone mentions Sindhi pakora, don't just nod politely—think about that double fry, that crispy texture, and the joy it's about to bring into your life. What's in a name? Everything. And this one? Pure, crispy perfection.

(Serves 3)

Ingredients

- 1 cup onions, diced into ½ inch cubes (the crunch factor)
- ¾ cup gram flour
- 1 tsp cumin seeds
- 2 medium green chillies, finely chopped (for that perfect zing)
- Salt, to taste
- Red chilli powder (to your spice level)
- A handful of coriander leaves, finely chopped (freshness overload)
- A pinch of baking soda (for that fluff)
- Water (just enough to bring it all together)
- Cooking oil (for deep frying, because... crispiness)

Method

1. In a bowl, mix together all the ingredients—onions, gram flour, cumin seeds, green chillies, salt, red chilli powder, and chopped coriander leaves. Add the baking soda.
2. Add just enough water to make a thick, yet scoopable batter. You want it to stick together but not be runny.

Pro Tip

Add a teaspoon of hot cooking oil to the batter and mix it well. This will make the pakoras crispy and golden.

3. Heat oil in a deep pan or *kadhai* for frying. (You want it nice and hot)
4. Carefully drop spoonfuls of the batter into the hot oil. Don't crowd the pan.
5. Fry the pakoras on medium flame, turning them until they're golden brown on the outside. You'll hear that lovely sizzling sound as they cook.
6. Once they're almost done, remove them using a slotted spatula and let them cool down a bit. Now, here's the fun part: break the pakoras into halves to make them even crispier.
7. Pop them back into the oil for a second fry until they're dark golden brown and extra crunchy.
8. Drain them on paper towels to get rid of all that excess oil, and voilà, the pakoras are ready to be devoured.
9. Serve them immediately with a bowl of tangy green chutney to add a burst of flavour.

These sanna pakoras are the ultimate crispy snack. Hot, spicy, and perfectly golden—they'll be gone in a flash. Ready to dive into this crispy delight?

Hosting: The Art of Welcoming (and Goodbye-ing)

Both Amma and Mamma had hosting down to an art form, but oh, the drama of it all.

When guests arrived at my Tamilian household, it was less about the 'hello' and more about the ceremony of greeting them. Picture this: preparing for guests in Amma's house was like prepping for a temple visit—with a bit more glitter.

Out came the sacred silver tray, which was always stored under the temple altar. Where else would it be, right? This tray had two silver bowls, one for turmeric, the other for *kungumam* (vermilion). But wait—the drama doesn't stop there. Half an hour before the guests arrived, Amma would carefully arrange a string of jasmine flowers on the plate. If betel leaves were in season, in they

went. You'd also find a piece of *paaku* (arecanut)—*vethalai* paaku, as they are called together—a shiny one-rupee coin and a new blouse piece (because a lady guest *must* get a blouse piece, even if she's just there for some coffee).

The *pièce de résistance*? A coconut—but only if the guest was really important. Ladies first, of course. The men just got a hearty *vanakkam* and coffee or Horlicks if it was their lucky day.

One banana (or many, depending on how generous Amma felt that day) also took up pride of place on the tray.

And here's the kicker: this lavish welcome wasn't for the arrival of the guest but for their departure. When the guest was ready to leave, Amma would spring into action, offering this glittering silver tray of goodies to the lady guest. First, the lady would dab her finger in the turmeric and kungumam and ceremoniously mark her forehead. Then, with a flourish, she'd take the rest of the items, drop them into a small bag Amma had thoughtfully kept ready and be on her way.

But hold on. In my Sindhi household, the banana was not even an *unsung hero*—totally different vibes. The banana was treated like it had to meet a full list of criteria before being allowed to grace your plate. Not before curd, not after curd, not too ripe, not too raw, not in the evening, and *definitely* not in winter. And forget about offering it to guests—the banana was only eaten once it passed a rigorous round of inspection.

In contrast, the banana in Tamilian homes had honorary temple status. It wasn't just a fruit—it was a spiritual experience. We'd offer it at the altar every day, like fruit royalty. Overripe bananas? Oh, they were turned into *panchamrutham*—a sweet dish so delicious that it could almost make you forget about the rest of the meal. Small batches, because you only had a couple of overripe bananas anyway.

So, you see, hosting in both households came with its own set of unique and wildly different rules. But no matter how it went, the guests always left feeling full.

Panchamrutham: A Sweet, Divine Delicacy

(Serves 3)

Ingredients

- 2–3 overripe bananas, mashed (the sweeter, the better)
- 1 tbsp roughly powdered jaggery (hello, natural sweetness)
- 1 tsp raisins (little bursts of sweetness)
- A few crystals of sugar candy (*safed misri,* for a delicate, crunchy finish)
- A drizzle of honey

Method

1. In a bowl, mash those overripe bananas.
2. Add the powdered jaggery, raisins, honey and sugar candy crystals to the mashed bananas—mix it all together with a cheerful swirl.
3. Serve it up with just about anything (parathas, rice, or simply by itself as a divine treat).
4. The magic touch: This sweet goodness is first offered as *naivedyam* (a holy offering made to the gods) at the temple altar before it gets to delight our taste buds.

It's that simple. Panchamrutham—a quick, comforting, and sacred treat that brings a touch of sweetness and tradition to any meal. Sweet, divine, and totally irresistible.

We Tamilians, oh, we swear by our *pazham*. Sure, the dictionary says pazham just means fruit but in every Tamilian home, it's the banana. The sheer sacredness of the pazham could start a holy war if anyone dared to buy it from outside the trusted family *pazhakaran*—the banana vendor. Going rogue and picking up bananas from the local market was practically an act of rebellion. Who dared? Certainly not a true-blue Tamilian!

Now, when you compare the Tamilian and Sindhi households, it's like comparing Mars to Venus. We were practically living in different galaxies. For starters, Amma's morning ritual involved a gigantic pot of coffee decoction— *'digagtion'* (try saying it with the appropriate flourish, a little bit of Sivaji Ganesan, if you please). This was not just any coffee, mind you. Filter coffee *was* sacred. Instant coffee? Don't even think about it. That's reserved for lazy souls and, more likely than not, non-Tamilians. No Tamilian worth their thayir sadam would ever disgrace their taste buds with that atrocity.

An hour before the guests arrived, the *upma* would be simmering away on the stove. On regular days, it had onions. But on *ammavasai* (the sacred no-onion days), the upma was onion-free—pure, simple, and as spiritual as the moonless night itself. By the time the evening rolled around, tiffin was the way to go. Tiffin—now that's *our* version of the Sindhi *nashto*.

Of course, no upma could dare enter your hands without a shiny steel *davara* (saucer-like dish) and tumbler of hot, steaming filter *kaapi* on the side. It wasn't just a drink; it was a ritual. But, here's the plot twist: some days, you'd find the healthy Bournvita or Horlicks sneaking in as the drink of choice, especially for the older crowd.

Filter Kaapi: The Elixir of Life (and Rebellion)

Every Tamilian household wakes up to the heady aroma of fresh coffee decoction—pronounced with a dignified 'digagtion,' of course. This isn't just coffee; this is the nectar that the rest of the world is still scrambling to find. In Amma's household, this divine concoction came from a packet boldly labelled Mysore Concerns Filter Coffee. During our early days in Bombay (yes, that's what it was called back then), our most prized possession—our kaapi *podi* (coffee powder)—could only be sourced from the holy land of Matunga, aka mini–Tamil Nadu.

It was Appa's sacred duty to pick up the coffee podi after work. If for some reason he failed (don't ask me how, but it happened), I had to step in, leaving college early just to make this holy pilgrimage. By the time I reached home, the warmest of welcomes was reserved not for me but for the prized coffee packet in my bag. Forget about my dramatic entrance—this was the real drama.

Fast forward to today, the mystical podi is easily found at my local Marwari grocer—who, if you ask me, probably has no idea what he's selling. Yet, Appa's ritual to get it remains nothing short of a religious journey. It's like walking up a hill to fetch water that tastes like the gods themselves brewed it.

Now, Mamma's household, on the other hand, would have laughed at this ritual. Coffee was something you only indulged in at fancy restaurants—mostly for the spectacle of it. It was what the elite drank, and they had no idea what they were missing. The common folk, however, were all about the chai, a drink that the British can sulk over, but we've already accepted as truth.

Amma would proudly serve her filter kaapi in a shining steel tumbler and davara (yes, *always* the tumbler and davara). Meanwhile, Mamma would serve tea in delicate, painted floral china cups she referred to as 'cope'. That word, cope, always carried more layers than a book of philosophy. There was *elaichi* (green cardamom). There was ginger. And there was a whole universe of emotions wrapped up in that tiny cup.

As the two mothers spent more time together, a strange, lovely thing began to happen. Mamma, the diehard chai lover, began to ask me to make coffee for Amma and Appa whenever they visited. The problem? I didn't own a coffee filter (I know, I know, utter sacrilege). What did I do? I bought the next best thing—Nescafé instant coffee—and brewed up a bland, watery potion. Amma, ever the sweet soul, would exaggerate how 'wonderful' it was, and Mamma would grin in approval. Some days, I think they secretly enjoyed making fun of me.

The irony, of course, was that when Mamma visited Amma, the coffee was never on offer—not even by oversight. Amma knew better. Without fail, tea was always ready for Mamma, served with the perfect touch, in a teacup and saucer, as if it were a special ritual just for her. There was no need for a word or a request—tea was Mamma's, always.

Such was the level of understanding, of quietly adapting to each other's preferences and choices. It wasn't just about the tea, of course—it was about the love in those small gestures. The way Amma remembered, even without being told, what would make Mamma feel most at home. It was bonding taken to a different level, where the act of offering tea wasn't just a routine—it was a beautiful testament to years of friendship, mutual respect, and the quiet language of care.

Every cup of tea served was a reminder that, sometimes, it's the simplest things that speak the loudest in a friendship. And in their case, it was a bond that went beyond words, beyond customs—it was a bond that was as warm as the tea itself.

Things have changed, though, in a way that still feels a bit surreal. Amma no longer knows how to make her beloved coffee decoction. It's a truth that hits like a quiet storm. The woman who once effortlessly brewed the perfect cup, who knew the exact timing, the perfect amount of water, and that precise touch, now watches from the sidelines.

Now, Appa takes the reins, waking up before the sun has even fully risen and brewing the coffee. He stands there in the kitchen, methodically pulling off the magic she once held so dear, the one ritual that defined her mornings. And Amma? She watches, utterly perplexed, her hands trembling just slightly as she sees him work his way through the process she once owned so completely. It's a bittersweet irony, one that's hard to swallow.

Appa's coffee—bless his heart—isn't quite there. It's missing that familiar depth, that soulful flavour Amma always got just right. It's not bad, but it's not quite the same.

So, now, in my own kitchen, I've embraced the sacred ritual. A sturdy brass filter lives in the cupboard alongside a packet of Mysore Concerns coffee podi. Every evening, two cups of piping hot filter coffee make their way across the lift lobby to Amma's house. Just imagine the stories that coffee could tell—it's like a historical novel in liquid form.

As for the switch from tumbler to cup? Well, the truth is, Amma's hands don't quite work the way they used to. The once-confident grip on the tumbler is now replaced by the steadier, more graceful hold of a cup. And maybe, just maybe, that's how things are meant to be.

Meanwhile, in Mamma's household, chai was what we woke up to. For guests? Chai was the drink you gave if you had nothing better to offer. But the real star of the show was always the *sharbat*—the famed *laal* sharbat. The drink was everywhere. Whether it was drizzled over *falooda*, blended with watermelon and crushed ice, or mixed into milk rose—this was the real Sindhi drink. You didn't need to serve it in a china cup, but in the hands of the right person it was always special.

When the bottle of laal sharbat threatened to run dry, Mamma would don her apron like a chef preparing for battle. With a glint in her eye and a mischievous smile, she'd march to the kitchen, ready to whip up a fresh batch—because when it comes to laal sharbat, there was no such thing as too much, only just enough *to last the day*.

Laal Sharbat from Red Roses

(Fills up a 1 ltr bottle)

Ingredients

- 6 cups of water
- ½ kg of rose petals (fresh, obviously. Don't even think about using old ones)
- 8 cups of granulated sugar (yes, *that* much—this is no place for subtle sweetness)
- 1 tbsp of lemon juice (for that tangy kick)
- A drop of red food colour (it's not just for drama, but it certainly helps)
- A few drops of rose essence (because subtlety is a myth)

Method

1. In a thick-bottomed pan, combine water, sugar and rose petals. Stir it with a confidence that says, 'I know what I'm doing,' and bring it to a boil.
2. Keep at it until the concoction reaches a thin string consistency—the kind that makes you feel like snapping your fingers.
3. Strain it like you're filtering out the mundane from your life and let it cool.
4. Pour this divine liquid into bottles and don't you dare let it sit in the fridge for too long. It's meant to be consumed immediately.

To Serve the Sharbat

Take a spoonful of the syrup, add it to a glass of ice-cold water (or milk, if you're feeling adventurous). Stir with the enthusiasm of someone who's about to witness the transformation of a simple drink into a masterpiece.

You must know, this milk rose is a favourite in the Sindhi community. It's in every household. They drink it through the summer months, and truly come across as pretty cool.

But wait—before the sharbat makes its grand debut at the table, picture this: the guests lounging lazily, backs supported by embroidered sofa covers, as Yera glasses glisten with fresh water. And on a silver tray, a china bowl cradles the choicest dry fruit, while Marie biscuits sit as the unassuming stars of the spread.

This is merely the opening act. The real show begins with a parade of aloo tikki, bread rolls, dahi vada and canapés—each dish more tempting than the last. But the one thing that reigns supreme, as constant as the stars in the sky, is the green chutney. Always. Forever.

The guests usually bring one—or all—of the following, as if their entry into your home isn't grand enough already:

1. A ½ or 1 kg box of kaju katli, wrapped in gleaming, almost criminally shiny cellophane. The kind of wrapping that makes you wonder if the cellophane itself is part of the gift.
2. A box of assorted dry fruit, where the same cellophane makes a dramatic reappearance. It's like the dry fruits are throwing a fancy party and the cellophane is their exclusive VIP pass.
3. A box of atte ke ladoo (wheat ladoo) and yes, wrapped in cellophane. Because nothing says 'I'm a sophisticated guest' like laddoos wrapped in what could be mistaken for a high-end fashion accessory.

God forbid the guest forgets the cellophane; it's practically sacrilegious. The unwrapping ceremony is nearly as intense as the unboxing of the latest tech gadget.

Aloo Love: From Simple to Sensational

Potatoes in Amma's kitchen were the rare guest star—like that elusive celebrity who only graces the screen every once in a while. If it was on the menu, you could bet it was making an appearance in the form of *podimas*—a one-pot wonder of mashed potatoes spiked with rai, curry leaves, and a dash of love. But outside of that? Potatoes were treated with the kind of reverence reserved for rare treasures—honoured, but rarely put to work.

Now, in Mamma's Sindhi kitchen, potatoes were like the backbone of the entire operation—omnipresent and unrelenting. In fact, they weren't just a food; they were practically a family member. Aloo paratha, bread rolls, tikkis, and sabzis—if there was a meal, the potato was the VIP guest, strutting across the table like it owned the place. In Mamma's kitchen, if you didn't see a potato, you'd wonder if you'd been dropped into a different universe. Here, it always pulled its weight.

But then there was the *urulaikizhanga* curry—the singular exception in Amma's kitchen, where potatoes made a fleeting cameo in a curry. This wasn't your everyday spud. Boiled, cubed, sautéed in ghee with a chorus of spices like urad dal, rai, and dried red chillies; it was a side dish that turned heads. A fleeting tribute to the potato, but once it was gone, it was back to its 'used only once in a while' status.

But hold onto your tastebuds—there was a time when roasted potatoes ruled Amma's kitchen, and it became the household's soul food. Enter the chapter where Appa, a daring telecommunications engineer with a newly minted sense of adventure, took the family to Zambia. This was the moment that roasted potatoes became Amma's masterpiece.

It all started in Lusaka, where Amma, already pregnant with my baby brother, was rushed to the hospital, labour pains in full swing. The diagnosis? False labour. But the Indian hospitality in Lusaka saved the day, offering us a roof over our heads before we flew to Kitwe. A month later, baby brother made his dramatic entrance into the world and just 24 hours later, Amma, still groggy, was discharged from the hospital, with him in her arms.

And then came the sprawling room in a guesthouse in a new neighbourhood of the town of Kitwe. Nothing—absolutely nothing could have prepared Amma for the sheer culinary horror of the canteen downstairs, which offered only boiled potatoes, peas, and carrots to vegetarians. Potatoes became her lifeline.

Fast forward to our new mansion in Kasama. The kitchen came with an in-built cooking range with a grill and oven. Appa went to work, but it was Amma and Michael, our ever-faithful houseboy, who got creative in the kitchen. Before long, our mouths were watering at the sizzling promise of roasted potatoes. Amma would dice the spuds, jacket and all, brush them with rich New Zealand butter, sprinkle them with salt and chilli powder, and slide them into the oven.

A mere 15–20 minutes later, and those potatoes would be the stuff of legend—crispy, golden, and melting in your mouth. Paired with hot rice and rasam. There was no better meal. Trust me.

Podimas: The Spicy South Indian Delight

Where humble potatoes get their sass and swagger, all thanks to a bit of coconut oil and an explosion of spices.

(Serves 3)

Ingredients

- 2 large potatoes (don't even think about skipping this)
- 1 onion, finely chopped
- 3 green chillies (go bold)
- ¼ cup freshly grated coconut (the game-changer)
- 1 tbsp coconut oil (it's that fancy touch we all crave)

For Tempering

- 2 tsp oil (don't skimp)
- ½ tsp rai (for that satisfying pop)
- 1 tsp urad dal (for the crunch, you'll thank me later)
- 1 sprig curry leaves (the scent that makes everything better)

Method

1. Chop that onion finely and slice your green chillies into those perfect little rings (we're here to impress).
2. Pressure cook those halved potatoes on high flame till you hear three satisfying whistles. Once done, peel off the skin and crumble those potatoes like you're a culinary master. No mashing here, just a gentle crumble (we're keeping it real).
3. Heat your kadhai with oil. Now, toss in the rai and let them sizzle and pop like you're at a fireworks show. Then, drop in the urad dal and roast it till it's golden crisp—let it snap and crackle like it's trying to make an entrance.

4. Add those curry leaves next and give them a quick fry till they release their aroma. Then toss in the onions and green chillies, sautéing till the onions become soft and transparent, but for heaven's sake, don't let them change colour. Keep it delicate. Add more oil if you need to keep the show going.
5. Add salt like you mean it, and then—brace yourself—tip in your glorious potato crumble. Stir like you're swirling magic into a cauldron.
6. Now, bring in the grated coconut for that rich, tropical crunch. Mix it all together and if you're feeling fancy, drizzle a little extra coconut oil for the grand finale.
7. Turn off the heat, take a moment to bask in the glory of what you've just created and then serve it hot, with some piping hot rice and rasam.

Aloo Tikki: Crispy On the Outside, Fiery On the Inside—Because Who Says Comfort Can't Be Spicy?

(Serves 6)

Ingredients

- 1 kg boiled and mashed potatoes (the fluffier the better—don't skimp)
- 4–5 green chillies, finely chopped (bring on the heat, baby)
- A sprig of fresh coriander, finely chopped (because, let's be real, it's what makes it look fancy)
- Half a cup of bread crumbs (get those edges crispy)
- Salt, to taste (don't be shy, we're not making porridge here)
- A dash of red chilli powder (add as much drama as you want)
- A pinch of garam masala (for that perfect, in-your-face punch)
- Oil for frying (whether you're shallow or deep, oil is the key to life)

Method

1. Knead it like you mean it—throw everything into a bowl and give it a good mix. Blend those spices into the potatoes like you're making the best damn mashed potatoes of your life.
2. Shape up—pinch a blob of that heavenly potato dough and pat it between your palms. Don't go all thin with the pat—make it thick and juicy. Tap the edges to smooth them out into a perfect circle. Set them aside like you're waiting for them to shine.

Shallow Frying (Mamma's way)

1. Heat up your tawa like you're about to make magic happen.
2. Grease it with a drop of oil—don't drown it, just a hint.
3. Place 5 or 6 tikkis on the tawa. Give them enough space to spread out like they own the place.
4. Drizzle a little oil around them—get the sides crispy.
5. Flip them when they're golden—don't be gentle, they can handle it.
6. Repeat the flip, making sure they're perfect on both sides.
7. Remove and drain on kitchen tissue—because these babies deserve a little rest.
8. Serve hot with, yep, green chutney. Because what else?

The Papad Perception: A Crisp Tale

Ah, the papad! The one food item that seems to have been unfairly tagged to the Sindhi community. I've always been amused by this misappropriation. Growing up surrounded by endless tins of pappadams and appalams, I can say with confidence—no one, absolutely no one, out-papads the Tamilians. The Sindhis may have earned the title, but we—well, we're the papad connoisseurs.

Let's get real here: My little reality check into the Sindhi side of the family—and trust me, it was an eye-opener—proved that papad-making became a lifeline for the Sindhi community post-partition. While the displaced Punjabis had a state to call their own, the Sindhis were left to piece together their lives from scratch. And here's where the papad enters: what started as a survival tactic—making and selling papads—transformed into a livelihood. So, while the tag sticks, I like to think that it's more out of necessity than passion. It was the hustle of survival, really.

But let's not forget: the papad is a national treasure. A staple across every region of India, it's a food item that transcends boundaries. The South Indian pappadam, made from rice and urad dal, is a crunchy delight, but the north has its own variations made of *sabudana* (sago pearls), potato and other starches. As for my Tamil household? We've hoarded Ambika appalam like it's some sort of sacred relic. Every other day, you'll hear the sizzle of these crisp discs dropping into bubbling oil, transforming into the perfect accompaniment to anything—be it rice and sambar, rasam, curd,

payasam or even a steaming cup of filter coffee. Yes, coffee—it's a thing.

And don't even get me started on the subtle yet distinct difference between pappadam and appalam. Pappadam puffs up like it's ready for a party thanks to its soda content, while the appalam stays resolutely flat. Both are gobbled up without a second thought in my Tamil household, but in my Sindhi world? The papad is a random guest. It makes an appearance, maybe once or twice a year.

Take winters, for instance. When *gajar halwa* makes its annual appearance in massive quantities, that's when the roasted papad makes its brief but glorious cameo, perfectly balancing the sweetness of the halwa with its savoury crunch. Sweet and savoury—a combination so genius, it almost feels like a conspiracy.

So, let's be clear: While the Sindhis may have pioneered the papad trade out of necessity, it's the Tamilians who've mastered the art of consumption, turning it into a daily ritual, an obsession. Papad? It's not just a food item; it's a lifestyle.

O, Sweet Rice

Sweet dishes abound in both kitchens, but if there's one dish that truly united the two mothers in their shared love for the sacred and the sweet, it's the humble, proletariat rice. It wasn't just any rice—it was the sweetened rice that carried the weight of tradition and ritual in both households. A dish that marked every festive day, no matter how big or small and was always offered to the gods as a humble, sugary offering.

Now, if you think that sweet rice is just rice with sugar, let me tell you, the Tamilian and Sindhi versions have their own secrets. But the true beauty of this dish lies not just in its taste, but in the rituals surrounding it, rituals that reveal more about the mothers who made it than the dish itself.

Amma's prayers were no small affair. Her devotion was an art form, a daily symphony of reverence and discipline. It began before the sun even thought of rising. First, there was the temple-cleaning ritual—no, not the temple down the road, but the one in her own home. A dusting of the sacred spaces, anointing the altar, followed by a *kolam* at the entrance. Her fingers, deft and familiar with the rice flour patterns, would draw intricate, geometric designs outside the door, all while her lips muttered shlokas and chants. She didn't even need to look up. Questions from us, mere mortals, were answered with a nod of the head or a simple gesture of the hand, but her mouth—oh no, that stayed occupied, a sacred channel for her prayers.

Despite her fervent devotion, Amma rarely set foot in a temple. 'My temple at home is enough,' she'd proclaim with the quiet confidence of someone who knew their path. A temple, after all, was in the heart, not just a building.

Mamma, on the other hand, had a more pragmatic approach to her prayers. Her rituals were brief and functional, an easy rhythm of daily life. A post-bath lighting of the lamp, a quick incense stick, here and there. But when it came to temple visits? That was where the heart and soul came alive. The process of selecting the perfect saree, the matching accessories, the right mood—everything was considered. And when she returned from the temple, her arms would be laden with *prasad*—not just for us—but for Amma too. 'Blessings are meant to be shared,' she'd always say with a smile, passing on her spoils like the generous soul she was.

And so it went, prasad made on festive days would shuttle back and forth between the homes. One constant, ever-present player in this ritual exchange was the tairi from Mamma's Sindhi kitchen and the *sakkarai pongal* from Amma's Tamilian one. The tairi, sweet, spiced, and aromatic, represented the Sindhi essence—fluffy rice simmered with black cardamom and cloves, a simple yet profound tribute to the gods. And then there was the sakkarai pongal, with its creamy rice, jaggery sweetness and ghee richness—an offering from Amma that was always made with love and devotion, in the heart of her kitchen.

Both dishes were far more than mere food. They were the tangible representations of devotion, the offerings that connected the earthly to the divine and the sweet link between two different worlds, coming together in one shared, sacred moment.

Tairi: Sweet and Spicy Rice, for When You're Feeling Fancy (or a Little Nostalgic)

(Serves 3)

Ingredients

- 2 cups basmati rice (make sure it's aromatic enough to make your neighbours, in our case Amma, curious)
- 1 cup jaggery (because sugar is too mainstream)
- 2 cups water (no, this isn't an ocean, just enough to make the rice swim)
- 4–5 black cardamom pods—for that exotic touch
- ½ tsp saunf (aka fennel seeds—because life is too short for boring spices)
- 4 tbsp kopra (dry coconut), sliced thin—thin enough to make you feel like a gourmet
- A pinch of kesar (saffron)—the golden ticket to flavour town
- 4 tsp ghee (because what's life without a little decadence)

- A pinch of green cardamom powder (yes, we're doubling down on the cardamom)
- A pinch of salt (it's elementary, Dr Watson)
- Raisins and assorted dry fruit for garnishing (because we're extra like that)

Method

1. Soak the rice for about 30 minutes—let it get cozy, like it's at a spa.
2. Slice up your jaggery into pieces so it can melt and do its sweet magic in the water.
3. Grab a sipri. Pour in the water and dissolve the jaggery in it like you've got all the time in the world. Add in those fennel seeds and black cardamom—don't rush this. It's about creating an aromatic symphony.
4. Toss in the rice and let it boil—yes, we're doing this the old-fashioned way, with the rice simmering slowly.
5. As the water evaporates, watch your rice bloom. It's almost time to make it rain raisins and dry coconut.
6. Lower the flame, cover it, and let the magic happen for a few minutes until the rice is cooked to perfection.
7. Now, heat up the ghee in a small pan—let it sizzle with the cardamom powder and dry fruits, then pour this golden goodness over your rice like you're sprinkling fairy dust.
8. Serve it hot and don't forget to relish it like it's a secret you're dying to share with the world.

Tairi—sweet, spicy, and definitely not your average rice. Serve this at any gathering and watch people scramble for seconds (and maybe thirds).

Sakkarai Pongal: Sweet Southern Comfort in a Bowl

(Serves 3)

Ingredients

- ½ cup rice (don't skimp on the quality—this is the foundation of your deliciousness)
- 2 tbsp yellow moong dal (split yellow gram, or the secret to soft, silky pongal)
- ¾ cup jaggery (no substitutions here, this is the gold standard)
- 2½ cups water (the amount of magic liquid your rice and dal need to cook up perfectly)
- 3 tbsp ghee (because ghee makes everything better, don't even argue)

- A pinch of salt (it's like a little wink in the dish)
- 6 cashews (toasted to golden perfection, for who doesn't love that crunch)
- 2 tbsp raisins (they're here for sweetness and a little squish)
- 1 green cardamom pod (the aromatic wonder)
- 1 clove (it adds that little 'what's that extra something' factor)
- 1 pinch of nutmeg powder (don't go too wild, just a dash)
- A tiny piece of edible camphor (yes, it's a thing, and it's magical)

Method

1. In a pressure cooker or pan, heat ¼ tablespoon of ghee and roast the moong dal until it smells toasty, like a warm hug.
2. Add water, the washed rice, and a pinch of salt—then pressure cook for 4 whistles. Once it's done, mash it up like you're channelling your inner chef.
3. In a separate pan, take your jaggery and powder it. Add a splash of water just to cover it and bring it to a gentle boil. Let the jaggery dissolve completely and then strain it (goodbye impurities) before adding it to your mashed rice.
4. In the same pan, heat 1 teaspoon of ghee. Roast the cashews until golden and toss in the raisins. When they puff up, transfer them to a plate and set aside.
5. In the same pan (don't clean it, keep that ghee flavour alive), toss in the cloves and the cardamom. Switch off the stove and let the spices do their thing.
6. Sprinkle in the nutmeg powder and stir it all together—oh, the smell is heavenly already.
7. Now, take the cardamom, powder it up and add it, along with the camphor, cloves, and nutmeg, to the pongal. Stir it like you're stirring in some love.
8. Let this simmer on medium flame for about 5 minutes. If it gets dry, don't panic—just add a little water or milk to keep it smooth and creamy.
9. Add the ghee in stages—don't rush it. Let each spoonful melt into the dish before you add more.
10. Lastly, toss in the roasted cashews and raisins and serve this warm, gooey, fragrant delight.

Sakkarai pongal—sweet, spiced and wrapped in nostalgia. Serve it at any festivity and watch it disappear within seconds.

Chhole Treat: The Annual Culinary Showdown

Ah, the sacred restaurant outing. For most people, dining out is a regular affair, but for us? It was a once-in-a-blue-moon extravaganza. The two occasions we were graced with a trip to a restaurant were as follows:

1. My birthday or my siblings' birthdays, which, let's be honest, were less about us and more about ensuring the adults didn't have to cook.
2. When a relative from down South came to visit and after a full day of sightseeing, eating out was the only 'logical' next step.

These outings were treated like high-stakes negotiations. Amma and Appa would consult the menu in hushed tones, deep in deliberation, as if they were selecting the next prime minister. And heaven forbid, we, the innocent children, even think about suggesting—'this' or 'that' on the menu? Amma's eyes would balloon to the size of frisbees and the conversation would abruptly stop, as if a thunderclap had just happened. We'd shrink back into our seats.

But, let's be real here. The first dish on the menu? Never up for debate: *chhole* (chickpeas). That was a given, a permanent fixture on the table, like the laws of physics. Whether you liked it or not, it was happening.

Now, let's talk about chhole in my Tamilian household. It was like a mythical creature—rarely seen and when it was, we treated it like a special guest. The closest we ever got to *kondakadalai* (chhole/white chickpeas) at home was during Navaratri and even then, it wasn't the spiced, gravy-coated chhole we dreamed of. Nope, it was *sundal*. Now, sundal might sound fancy, but in reality, it's boiled chickpeas dressed up like they were going to a five-star party. We'd get sundal during Navaratri, when Amma would set up an elaborate display of deity figurines, golu and suddenly, the humble chickpea would be transformed into this tangy, spicy, mouth-watering treat.

But, let's not forget my childhood outings with Thatha (Appa's father) to Marina Beach in Chennai, which were a whole other level of 'spicy.' Thatha would walk me along the beach, explaining life's great mysteries while we enjoyed paper-coned servings of sundal and *mangai* (raw mangoes sprinkled with a devilish amount of chilli powder and salt). The real kicker? These paper cones were torn out of old magazines. Nothing says 'authentic' like MGR, Sivaji Ganesan, and K. R. Vijaya staring at you from their glossy, black-and-white faces, while your lips are on fire from the sundal. It was practically a religious experience—except you were more likely to pray for water than for divine intervention.

Ah, memories. Some were of chhole at the restaurant. Some were of sundal on the beach. Both equally satisfying, though I'll admit: the sundal did have more gravitas.

Sundal: The Beachside Delight, Now in Your Kitchen

Ah, sundal—the quintessential beach snack that makes you feel like you're experiencing a taste of divine intervention, even if you're just sitting at your kitchen counter in your pyjamas. This is no ordinary chickpea dish. It's the flavour-packed snack that brings the magic of Marina Beach right to your home. Prepare to transport your taste buds straight to Chennai, where the salty sea breeze and the spicy kick of sundal make for a match made in snack heaven.

(Serves 3)

Ingredients

- 1 cup kondakadalai—because why settle for anything less than the mighty chickpea?
- 3–4 cups water (for the all-important pressure-cooking stage that'll leave you with soft, tender chickpeas ready for their big moment)

- 2 tbsp oil (we're talking the good stuff to bring out that flavour)
- 1 tsp rai (for that crunchy pop of flavour—maybe even a little dance party in your pot)
- 1 tsp urad dal—because what's a South Indian snack without the crunch of dal?
- A pinch of asafoetida—the secret weapon that makes everything magically delicious
- 2 dried red chillies (broken, seeds removed)—or you could swap it for 1 to 2 green chillies if you're feeling bold and a little zesty

- 10–12 curry leaves—essential, as without them, you might as well be serving plain boiled chickpeas
- 2–3 tbsp freshly grated coconut—the kind that transforms your dish from 'meh' to 'wow!'
- Salt, to taste (because no dish is complete without the perfect seasoning)

Method

1. The night before your big sundal adventure, let the chickpeas soak in water, like they're at a luxurious spa retreat. Let them relax and soften up. The next day, rinse and give them a little bath of fresh water.
2. Place your soaked chickpeas in the pressure cooker, along with 1 teaspoon of salt and 3–4 cups of water. Cook those babies for about 12–15 minutes on medium heat (or more, if you're feeling generous). When the chickpeas are tender and soft, drain all the water and set them aside. *Patience is key here*—good things take time.
3. Heat oil in a pan, and add the rai and urad dal. Let them cook together on a low flame—this is where the magic happens. You'll know you're doing it right when the rai starts popping like fireworks, and the dal turns golden brown.
4. Once the flavours have come together nicely, let's kick it up a notch. Add the curry leaves, broken red chillies, and a pinch of asafoetida.

Fry everything together for 10–15 seconds, or until the curry leaves get nice and crispy.

5. Toss in your cooked chickpeas with a generous pinch of salt. Stir it all up and let it simmer for 3–4 minutes on low to medium heat. You want the flavours to mingle like a great party.
6. With a flourish, switch off the heat, and finish off by adding the fresh grated coconut, giving everything one last stir. You've just created a magical, mouth-watering sundal that could make even the most sceptical person believe in the power of chickpeas.

Now, you have the option to serve your sundal as prasad or naivedyam to the deities, because let's be honest—this dish is practically blessed. Or, if you're not feeling particularly spiritual, serve it as a snack at your next party. It'll be a hit, no questions asked.

If you want to take it to the next level, channel your inner Thatha and serve it in a paper cone with a side of raw mango sprinkled with chilli powder. Ah, bliss.

So, now you can enjoy the taste of sundal whenever you want—whether you're at the beach, at a temple, or simply curled up on your couch binge-watching your favourite show. Sundal, the snack that brings the world to your doorstep, one spicy bite at a time.

The Street Food Revelation: A Tamilian's Take

Street food? What's that? Growing up in my Tamilian household, we didn't have the luxury of indulging in the kind of street food others raved about. The closest we got was sundal on the beach or the occasional peanuts sold at traffic signals. Sure, it's got a 'street food' vibe, but let's be honest: peanuts and sundal didn't have the same, *ahem*, allure as the *chaats* and *chaap chhola* that were popular in other parts of India. And I secretly suspected, after a lot of intense pondering, that food which could not first be proffered as naivedyam to the gods in our home altar was clearly not meant for human consumption. No divine approval? No eating. Simple as that.

My earliest memories of food are linked to the smell of fresh milk. The day would start with this scent, always coming from the designated little pot—a vessel so tiny it looked like something out of a dollhouse kitchen, made of shiny silver that gleamed in the early morning light. Amma would pour the freshly boiled milk into this pot with a reverence that would make even the gods blush. Then, with all the seriousness of a priest preparing for an ancient ritual, she'd take it to the altar. There, she'd offer it up to the gods—praying for their divine approval, begging them to take a sip. Of course, they never did, but that didn't stop

Amma from treating the moment as if the gods were about to hold a royal banquet.

After the milk's brief spiritual 'sip,' Amma would carefully bring the pot back to the kitchen, pour it back into the main milk vessel and give it a good stir. Then came the all-important, solemn nod from Amma, 'Good to drink now that it's been blessed.'

But then came the day—oh, that unforgettable day—when I watched a movie where food was served to a king, but before he took a bite, the servant tasted it. The servant gave a nod of approval and only then did the king partake. My mind was blown. I spent a good number of nights trying to figure out the power dynamics between the gods and Amma. Shouldn't it have been the other way around? Shouldn't she have been testing the milk before the gods could drink it?

It took me several years to realise that young (read: overly philosophical) minds don't always get answers to deep questions. Sometimes, you just have to accept that your mother is a goddess in her own right—and if she says the milk's blessed, then by all means, drink up.

So, street food? Nah. Not in my house. We had milk ceremonies and offerings to the gods. And, sure, while I couldn't quite grasp the divine logic back then, I eventually understood one thing: my house wasn't just a home—it was an altar to tradition.

Chaap Chhola: A Sindhi Street Food Legend

In my Sindhi household, chhole were not just a regular item—they were an absolute street food sensation. But, let's be honest, every Sindhi will proudly tell you that *the best* chhole experience happens not in the comfort of your kitchen, but at the local roadside chaap chhola vendor. And no, we're not talking about any fancy restaurant dish here. We're talking about the magical concoction whipped up at the bustling street food carts, or *thelo*, as they're affectionately known in Sindhi.

This tangy, zingy, utterly lip-smacking dish is the true heartbeat of Sindhi street food. Even today, a trip to Ulhasnagar—the Sindhi's very own mini-metropolis—would be incomplete without a steaming plate of chaap chhola from a thela. Whether it's the bustling streets of Ulhasnagar or the lively hubs in Sindhi-dominated areas across the country, the chaap chhola reigns supreme.

Here's the kicker: the street vendors, the ones who once pushed carts, have transformed into culinary legends. You'll find them now owning some of the most illustrious, finger-licking restaurants around the country. A true rags-to-riches tale—proof that no one can quite make chaap chhola like the people who've lived and breathed it for generations.

But enough of the nostalgia—let's get down to the business of recreating the dish at home, because who doesn't want to take a little slice of street-food heaven to their own kitchen?

Chhola: The Tangy Magic

(Serves 3)

Ingredients

- 2 cups boiled kabuli chana (chickpeas)—because we want those peas perfectly tender to soak up all the deliciousness
- 2 onions, finely chopped (these will form the golden base of your curry)
- 2 tsp ginger-garlic paste (for that irresistible depth of flavour)
- 6 tomatoes, pureed (the juicy base of the gravy)
- 1 tsp red chilli powder (we like a little heat in our chhole)
- 2 tsp coriander powder (a must for that warm, earthy touch)
- ½ tsp turmeric powder (because we need that golden colour)
- 1–2 tsp black salt (the secret ingredient that gives it that irresistible tang)
- 2 tsp chhole masala (No chhole is complete without this magical spice mix)
- ½ tsp garam masala (for that extra depth)
- ¼ tsp black peppercorns (to round out the flavours)
- Fresh coriander leaves (to garnish and add that fresh pop)

Method

1. Heat oil in a pan.
2. Add onions and sauté until they're pink and start to soften.

3. Add ginger-garlic paste and sauté until the onions turn deep golden (don't rush this part—this is where the flavour magic happens).
4. Add the tomato puree and all your spices. Let it simmer until all the moisture from the tomatoes has evaporated and the oil starts separating.
5. Add water to adjust the consistency and let it cook for another 10 minutes. You want a lovely runny gravy that your chhole can soak up.

Chaap: The Potato Patty Perfection

Ingredients

- 4 boiled potatoes (the starchy base for your chaap)
- 2 slices of bread (these will act as a binder and help hold everything together)
- salt, to taste (because, well, we all know the importance of seasoning)

Method

1. Mash the boiled potatoes until smooth.
2. Soak the bread slices in water for a few minutes, then squeeze them out thoroughly.
3. Crumble the soaked bread and mix it into the mashed potatoes.
4. Add salt and knead the mixture like dough. You want everything to come together into a smooth, firm texture.

Stuffing: The Heart of the Chaap

Ingredients

- ½ cup chana dal (the perfect filling to bring the dish together)
- 1 small onion, finely chopped (for that crunch and texture)
- 2 green chillies (because a little heat never hurt anyone)
- ¼ tsp aamchur (dry mango powder for that zingy punch)
- ¼ tsp turmeric

- ¼ tsp red chilli powder (more heat, you're welcome)
- A pinch of garam masala (to finish things off with warmth)
- Fresh coriander leaves (for that fresh, herbaceous finish)
- Salt, to taste (because flavour is key)

Method

1. Boil the chana dal with salt and turmeric until the grains are separate and tender.
2. Drain the excess water and let the dal cool.
3. Add the spices, green chillies, onion, and fresh coriander, then mix it all together. You want a well-combined, flavourful stuffing ready to roll.

Assembling the Chaap

1. Pinch out medium-sized balls from your potato dough.
2. Make a small depression in the centre of each ball and stuff 1 teaspoon of the chana dal filling into it.
3. Seal the sides, then flatten the ball into a patty.
4. Shallow fry or deep fry these patties until they turn golden and crispy on the outside, just like they should.

Gidamdi Ji Chutney: Tamarind Chutney to Elevate Everything

Ingredients

- A bunch of coriander leaves
- A small bunch of mint leaves
- 1 onion (to add a savoury base to the chutney)
- 4–5 green chillies (for that spicy kick)
- ½ cup diluted tamarind pulp (the tart base for your chutney)
- Salt, to taste (for that perfect balance)

Method

1. Grind coriander, mint, onion, green chillies, and salt into a smooth paste.
2. Add the tamarind pulp and adjust the consistency as needed. The chutney should be spicy and tangy, nothing less.

Accompaniments

- Fried green chillies (for those who like their spice level cranked up)
- Chopped onions (because no thela experience is complete without a sprinkle of raw onions)
- *Dabbal* or *pav* (the perfect vehicle for soaking up all that gravy and chutney)

Final Step

Serve and feast. In a shallow dish, place a chaap, pour a ladle full of the chhola, pour the chutney generously over the chhola, bring in the accompaniments. Now, you've got the ultimate chaap chhola—a combination of spicy, tangy, crispy, and absolutely addictive. Every bite is a journey, taking you straight to the streets of Ulhasnagar or wherever the thela vendors are serving up their magic. So, grab your plate, pour on that chutney, and enjoy the chaap chhola experience like never before. Who knew street food could taste this good—right in the comfort of your own home?

Give Us Today Our Daily Bread

Bread, or pav (the bun), might as well have been a foreign concept in my Tamilian household. It had zero mention in my memory album, nestled somewhere between 'rice' and 'sambar'. And yet, across the kitchen divide in my Sindhi household, the humble pav was a hero, a saviour on days when things didn't go as planned.

In Sindhi, pav is lovingly transformed into dabbal—which, if we're being literal, means 'double bread.' Why double, you ask? Well, isn't that what a bun is? Two slices of bread sticking together in the thick of it all? Also, that's just how things roll in the magical land of Sindhi linguistics. The etymology of Sindhi words can often leave you in stitches, especially when you start unpacking them. Take, for instance, the word slice. In Mamma's vocabulary, it was no ordinary 'slice.' Oh no. When she wanted one single slice of bread, she simply cut the '*ice,*' so to speak and proudly asked for a '*sli.*' But when she needed more than one, it was always, in full form, '*slice.*' That's right, one slice became 'sli,' and a few more slices morphed into slice. Mamma might not have been fluent in the Queen's English, but her shorthand? Spot on for survival.

Now, back to the dabbal—the unsung hero of every Sindhi meal. In our kitchen, the nomenclature dabbal and pav easily morphed into one another. Whichever way it was addressed, it was the saviour that would swoop in and rescue us from the dark depths of leftover gravies. The best part? It wasn't just limited to gravies; it had an uncanny ability

quick fix. Just grab a dabbal, dunk it into the dal and experience comfort in its purest form. There's no turning back once you get a taste of it.

to transform leftovers into something magically delicious. Leftover aloo tikkis? Pop them into a dabbal, slather on some green chutney, and voilà! You've got yourself a 'burst of flavours on your tongue' quick snack. Trust me, it's an art.

But that's not all. Are you tired of the same-old dal with rice or rotis? Enter the dabbal—the ultimate quick fix. Just grab a dabbal, dunk it into the dal and experience comfort in its purest form. There's no turning back once you get a taste of it.

And then, of course, there's the *pièce de résistance*—chaap chhola—a meal so irresistibly good that after the first bite, you'll find yourself reaching for more, not out of hunger, but sheer craving. The dabbal is the ultimate partner for this dish, soaking up all the spices and gravies like it was made for nothing else.

In my Tamilian kitchen, bread was a rare guest. But in the Sindhi one, it was the dependable star of the show, the ultimate kitchen sidekick that could take on gravies, tikkis, dal and anything else with sheer brilliance. You could always count on it to turn any meal into a comfort food fest, and honestly, that's a kind of magic that no other bread (read roti) can replicate.

Seyal Bread: An Explosion of Flavours

Lots of Pav and Nothing to Go with It? What Would Mamma Do Here?

Seyal bread is like the ultimate comfort food that comes to your rescue when you least expect it. When Mamma was faced with a lonely loaf of pav and a fridge full of nothing that could complement

Simple. Mamma would whip up a hearty plate of *seyal* bread—the Sindhi answer to everything that's left over but still worth rescuing. Picture this: a pile of pav just sitting there, looking all plump and ready, but with no gravy in sight. What's a girl to do? Seyal bread to the rescue.

it, she knew what to do. She'd turn it into an indulgent feast that we would devour till the last crumb. And don't even get me started on how the house would smell—just the right mix of spices and tomatoes, enough to make anyone hungry.

(Serves 3)

Ingredients

- Ladi pav (tear them up in large chunks, don't be shy)
- 4 ripe tomatoes (more the merrier)
- A generous sprig of coriander (cleaned, chopped, and fresh)
- 4–5 green chillies (or more, depending on your spice tolerance—don't blame me if your mouth catches fire)
- 7–8 garlic pods (yes, we're going all in with the garlic)
- Salt, to taste (use your judgement, we're not in the business of bland food)
- 1 tsp turmeric (just a pinch of sunshine)
- 1 tsp red chilli powder (for that extra kick)
- 1 tsp coriander-cumin powder (basically magic in powder form)
- 2 tbsp oil (because what's life without a little oil?)

Method

1. First things first, grab your grinder and turn those tomatoes, coriander, green chillies, and garlic into a fine, aromatic paste. This is the base of your seyal bread, and trust me, it smells divine already.
2. To the paste, toss in the magic—yes, the masala powders (turmeric, red chilli, and coriander-cumin powder) along with salt. Give it a mix and feel free to take a sneak sniff. You're in for a flavour bomb.
3. To sauté like a pro, start by heating the oil in a pan (medium flame, don't rush it) and then add the paste. Stir it around until the oil begins to separate from the paste. This is when you know you're doing it right.
4. For pav time, drop the chunks of pav into the masala paste and toss them around till they're generously coated with all the spicy goodness.
5. Lower the heat a bit, add about 2 spoons of water and mix well. Now, cover it with a lid and let it simmer for about 5 minutes. This will allow all the flavours to soak in, and you'll get that perfect, soft, yet slightly crispy texture that makes seyal bread so irresistible.

6. After the 5 minutes are up, give it one last stir and sprinkle some chopped coriander over the top for that fresh pop of colour and flavour, giving it that final touch.
7. Serve and enjoy this steaming hot, and watch it disappear faster than you can say 'leftovers.' You can even try it with leftover rotis, but let's be real, pav is always the star here. When made with rotis, the dish changes its name to seyal *maani* (roti).

Seyal bread is that dish that takes the simplest ingredients—old bread, some tomatoes, a few spices—and transforms them into a feast. A bit of oil, a dash of masala and voilà! You've got yourself a meal that makes you forget you were ever worried about what to do with the leftover pav. It's the perfect mix of tangy, spicy, and savoury, with a touch of nostalgia. It's not just food; it's magic in every bite.

Karela (Bitter Gourd): You Sweet Thing

Ah, the humble bitter gourd. The one thing both the mothers absolutely drooled over. Yes, bittersweet, isn't it? Yet, there was no rivalry here, no 'my recipe is better than yours'. Instead, both were thrilled by the idea of learning how the other prepared this underrated vegetable. Sadly, it has a limited fan base across the globe, but not in our kitchens.

Amma, a true fan of the bitter gourd, would delight in making her *pavakkai pitlai*. Since my dear hubby is a huge fan, Amma always made a generous portion for her son-in-law, sending it over with great pride. Mamma too would always indulge, nodding her approval after every spoonful.

But the true magic happened when Amma tasted Mamma's Sindhi *dhaage waara karela*. It was a sight to behold—the way the bitter gourds were slit in the middle, stuffed with onion and tomato masala, and neatly bound together with string. The presentation alone was enough to captivate anyone. Curious, Amma asked Mamma for the recipe. But soon enough, the complexity of the recipe and the language barrier left her feeling overwhelmed. After a couple of tries, Amma cheekily shrugged, 'Why should I bother? Whenever you make it, you'll send me some anyway,' and that was that.

Amma's pitlai was legendary. In fact, her son-in-law declared it the best in the world. Amma had a special connection with pitlai; the spicy, bittersweet curry paired perfectly with rice and she made it like no one else.

Mamma, on the other hand, always referred to the dish as 'karela sambar,' a term that tickled Amma every time. Yet, Amma never corrected her. It didn't matter whether the language was off or not. What mattered was the shared love for food. Food, after all, transcends all barriers—even language.

And thus, their bond over the humble bitter gourd continued to thrive.

Pavakkai Pitlai: A Bittersweet Symphony

(Serves 3)

Ingredients

- 2 large bitter gourds
- ½ cup tuvar dal
- Small lemon-sized tamarind ball (or 1 tsp paste)
- Salt, to taste
- 1 pinch turmeric powder

For Grinding

- ½ cup grated coconut
- 4 red chillies (adjust to your spice level)
- 3 tsp coriander seeds
- 2 tsp urad dal
- 2 tsp chana dal
- ½ tsp whole black peppercorns (optional)
- 2 tsp oil
- 1 sprig curry leaves
- ¼ tsp asafoetida

For Seasoning

- 1 tsp oil
- 1 tsp rai
- Some curry leaves

Method

1. Soak the tamarind in warm water for 10 minutes. Extract the juice and set aside.
2. Lightly peel the bitter gourd, remove the seeds, slice into roundels, and set aside.
3. Pressure cook the tuvar dal with turmeric for 4 whistles. Mash and keep aside.
4. Shallow fry red chillies, coriander seeds, urad dal, chana dal, and whole black peppercorns until golden. Then fry grated coconut, curry leaves and asafoetida until golden. Cool and grind everything into a fine paste.
5. Heat oil in a pan, add rai till it splutters, add some more curry leaves, and sauté. Add bitter gourd, stir-fry on medium heat

until it loses its bitterness, then cook with ½ cup water until soft and your seasoning is complete.

6. For cooking the pitlai, start by adding tamarind juice and salt. Boil for 5 minutes. Stir in the ground paste, mashed dal and adjust consistency with water. Let it boil once more before turning off the heat.
7. Combine the prepared seasoning with the pitlai and give it a good mix.
8. Serve and enjoy this bittersweet pitlai with hot, steaming rice.

Pro Tip

Amma added a small chunk of jaggery for the sweet edge.

A tantalising twist of bitterness, spice, and zest—pavakkai pitlai will make your tastebuds dance with joy.

Dhaage Waara Karela: The Bitter Comedy of Flavours

(Serves 3)

Ingredients

- 250 gm bitter gourd
- 3 medium-sized onions, finely chopped (for all the tears we'll be shedding)
- 2 ripe tomatoes, finely chopped
- A sprig of fresh coriander, cleaned and chopped
- 3–4 green chillies, finely chopped
- ¼ tsp turmeric (the golden touch)
- Red chilli powder (as per your heat endurance)
- Coriander-cumin powder (a dash of flavour, a burst of joy)
- Aamchur (for that zing)
- Salt, to taste
- Oil for cooking (don't skimp on this—it's for the sizzle)
- Clean white thread (for the bitter gourd's very own makeover)

Method

1. Start by lightly peeling the bitter gourd. Make it look nice and fresh for its big debut. Slit it vertically, scoop out the seeds (they're

not invited to the party). Rub salt all over the bitter gourds, inside and out. Let it sit for 1 hour. (This is where the bitterness takes its sweet leave.)

2. Heat some oil in a pan and drop in those green chillies and onions. Sauté until the onions start turning colour—they're giving us their best look. Add in the tomatoes and cook until they're no longer raw (they've got to be properly done for this epic meal).

3. Now, remove from the heat and toss everything into a bowl. Add in your spicy mix—turmeric, red chilli powder, coriander-cumin powder, aamchur and salt. Garnish with coriander, because who doesn't love a little green touch?

4. Wash the bitter gourds thoroughly and drain it (this helps get rid of the bitterness—don't want the bitterness stealing the spotlight). In the same pan, heat more oil and shallow

fry the bitter gourds until they turn golden brown. Let them cool off.

5. Stuff each bitter gourd with the onion-tomato filling. Now, tie a clean thread around each bitter gourd like it's getting ready for a runway show. This is some top-tier culinary fashion.

6. For the frying finale, heat a little oil in the same pan and gently drop in the stuffed bitter gourds. Shallow fry on high flame for 2–3 minutes—crisp and ready for the main event. Any leftover stuffing? Throw it around like confetti.

7. Lower the flame, cover the pan, and let the stuffed bitter gourds cook for about 10 minutes. Maybe add a few drops of water to prevent sticking at the bottom of the pan.

8. After 10 minutes, turn off the flame and get ready for the grand reveal. Our dish is ready to be served with rice and dal or hot rotis.

Note

Don't forget to untie the bitter gourds before eating—otherwise, well.

Now, who said bitter can't be beautiful? Dhaage waara karela, a dish with all the flavours and loads of chutzpah.

Sweet Meets Spice: A Tale of Two Vermicellis

Growing up, I believed *semiya* (vermicelli) was a purely Tamilian treasure. After all, Amma's iconic semiya *javvarisi* payasam—a creamy dessert of vermicelli and sago—was the crowning glory of every birthday lunch. I'd fish out the translucent sago pearls one by one, savouring their jelly like texture as my heart danced with joy.

So, imagine my surprise when, after getting married into a Sindhi household, I discovered semiya in an entirely new avatar. Enter *seyun*: a sweet, fragrant vermicelli dish, but with a surprising twist. Mamma paired it with spicy, shallow-fried potatoes. The combination of sugary comfort and fiery crispness was nothing short of exotic and unexpectedly delightful.

Two kitchens, two worlds, but one common ingredient that brought a burst of nostalgia and novelty to my plate.

Seyun Patata: The Sindhi Savoury Delight

(Serves 3)

Ingredients

- 1½ bowls of vermicelli (thin variety—yes, Mamma's twist on tradition)
- 2 tbsp cooking oil (I cheated by using ghee to elevate the drama)
- ½ cup sugar
- 3–4 potatoes, peeled, cubed, and parboiled

- ¼ tsp turmeric
- ½ tsp chilli powder
- Salt, to taste

Method

1. In a thick-bottomed pan, heat the oil. Lower the flame and add the vermicelli. Roast it till it's brown and glorious, but don't let it get too crispy.
2. Once the vermicelli is golden and the oil is absorbed, add just enough water to soak it (we're not drowning it, just giving it a cozy bath). Let it simmer on low flame till the vermicelli is cooked to perfection.
3. Add sugar and stir it all in to sweeten this deal. Keep cooking until the sugar dissolves and is fully absorbed. When it's all sticky and sweet, it's time to turn off the heat. Garnish with almonds, pistachios, and cardamom (this is optional—Mamma did not add any of it). Let it sit for a second so the magic can happen.
4. While the vermicelli is getting its moment, heat oil in another pan. Drop in those parboiled, cubed potatoes, and add turmeric, chilli powder and salt. Sauté until the potatoes are golden and well-coated in spices. Don't let them go mushy—we want a perfect bite.
5. Plate the vermicelli and serve it with the savoury potatoes as a side dish. The potatoes add that perfect crunch to the sweet, soft vermicelli—it's the ultimate balancing act.

Now, on to Amma's semiya javvarisi payasam—a showstopper.

Semiya Javvarisi Payasam: Vermicelli and Sabudana / Sago Delight

(Serves 3)

Ingredients

- ½ cup vermicelli
- ¼ cup javvarisi (sabudana/ sago pearls)
- 4 cups of milk
- ½ cup sugar (adjust to taste)
- 2 tbsp ghee
- 10–12 cashews
- 10–12 raisins
- ¼ tsp green cardamom powder
- A few strands of saffron, for that festive touch

Method

1. Rinse the sago well under running water. Soak them in enough water for 30 minutes to 1 hour, until they plump up. Drain and set aside.
2. Heat 1 tablespoon of ghee in a pan. Add the vermicelli and roast on low flame until golden and aromatic. Set aside.
3. In a saucepan, bring 2 cups of water to a boil. Add the soaked sago and cook for about 5–7 minutes, until they turn translucent. Drain and keep them ready.

4. In another pot, bring the milk to a gentle boil, stirring occasionally to prevent scorching. Add the roasted vermicelli and cook on low flame for another 5–7 minutes, until the vermicelli softens.
5. Stir in the cooked sago, sugar, cardamom powder and saffron. Simmer for another 5 minutes, allowing the flavours to meld beautifully.
6. Heat the remaining 1 tablespoon of ghee in a small pan. Fry the cashews until golden, then toss in the raisins until they puff up. Add this glorious garnish to the payasam.
7. Serve warm or chilled, depending on your mood. Each spoonful is a creamy, dreamy burst of nostalgia.

Pro Tip

For extra richness, you can substitute part of the milk with coconut milk or condensed milk. Enjoy this comforting treat that's equal parts tradition and indulgence.

Gobble, Gulp, Guzzle: A Study in Speed and Stereotypes

Classic *Elai Sapadu* Time: A 32-Course Meal in 15 Minutes Flat

For my family, food wasn't a leisurely affair. It was a necessary interruption to life's bigger happenings. Sure, it had its place of pride on the *elai* or the banana leaf (in Tamil households, the elai is the pinnacle of all dining experiences), but you didn't linger over it. You ate. You relished. You thanked the gods with a loud burp. And then, you were off to the next thing on the checklist.

In my Sindhi household, however, food was the glue that held everything together—disputes, disagreements, celebrations, condolences, marriage negotiations, you name it. All of it happened over *nashto*, maani, or *pyaala*s (bowls) of falooda.

Back in the day, when Sindhi relatives or friends dropped by for lunch or dinner, we didn't even bother with fancy tables. Nope. We spread out newspaper sheets—on the floor, on the bed—wherever there was space. It was an art form, really. The space was cramped, the chairs were too few, but everyone found a spot to perch. It wasn't about where you sat; it was about the company. And the finger-licking, of course. I distinctly remember sitting for hours, chatting and, yes, licking dry fingers. Not a moment of shame in sight.

Now, contrast that with my Tamilian household. Licking fingers was a crime punishable by a glare from Appa, whose expression could curdle milk. Appa was serious about eating. He ate like it was an Olympic sport—efficient, quick, and without a single morsel left behind. And the minute the last bite was swallowed, he would rise with the grace of a monk, hand behind his back, making a beeline for the bathroom. It wasn't over until the hand-washing ritual was complete. Only after he emerged, rubbing his hands dry on the cotton *thorthu* (traditional bath towel), did his face finally crack into a smile. 'Check!' the internal checklist would whisper. Only then, could he return to normalcy.

So, in a nutshell (or shall I say, in a full 32-course meal), in my Tamilian home, food culture was about precision and dignity. Across the lobby, Sindhi food culture was about chaos, love and… let's be honest… a whole lot of finger-licking. But, hey, what's family without a little spice?

Curd: The Battle of the Dairy Divas

The humble curd—let's talk about this dairy darling, shall we? In my Sindhi household, curd rarely made an appearance in its purest, most dignified form. Oh no, it preferred to keep things exciting with its variations—dahi vada, buttermilk, and the like. Curd was a fun, funky character at the party, popping in every now and then, but never as the main attraction.

In my Tamilian home, however, curd was revered like a deity. It was not just a condiment; it was practically worshipped. Amma's philosophy was clear: 'The sign of a big pot of thayir (curd) in the fridge is a sign of prosperity.' If you didn't have curd in your fridge, were you even living? It was the social status symbol of the kitchen, next only to the naivedyam. Setting the curd was a sacred ritual, involving specific utensils, a meticulously calibrated milk temperature, and, of course, the precise amount of curd required for the perfect set. And then, the curd had to be placed in its designated 'setting spot' (as if it were a VIP guest at a party).

My taste buds were so accustomed to finishing every meal with a lavish helping of curd—either as a stand-alone dish or elegantly perched on top of rice—that when I entered my Sindhi household, I was already mourning its absence by the first meal. Freshly minted hubby, eager to please, dashed to the grocer and bought a large cup of dahi for me. 'Here, darling' he said, presenting it like a treasure chest. 'This should do the trick!' I took a spoonful and remembered to set the curd that night, determined to bring some dairy magic into this new world.

By the next week, Mamma was reminding me every day to set the curd. And like clockwork, I bought a mud pot exclusively for the sacred task of setting curd. Prosperity soon overflowed in my fridge and it wasn't long before Mamma, the true curd convert, added a generous *katori* of curd to her lunch plate. My mission was accomplished.

But, despite my best curd-setting efforts, there was one thing that could never find a home in my Sindhi kitchen: mor kuzhambu. Oh sure, we gave it a shot a few times, but it just didn't click. The blend of yoghurt, spices and curry leaves simply didn't pass the Sindhi taste test. Except—drumroll, please—for Amma's *mambazham* mor kuzhambu. This royal version, made with Alphonso mangoes during mango season, floored my Sindhi family. Pair it with hot rice and appalam, and you attain nirvana.

So, while my Sindhi household may not have taken to any random mor kuzhambu like a duck to water, we did find a way to worship curd—and yes, prosperity was indeed served, one pot of curd at a time.

Mambazham Mor Kuzhambu: A Mango Tango of Flavours

(Serves 3)

Ingredients

- 3 or 4 ripe mangoes (the juicier, the better)
- 1 small cup of freshly grated coconut
- ½ inch ginger (for that zing)
- ¼ tsp turmeric powder (just a pinch, but make it count)
- 1 tsp coconut oil (trust me, it's the secret sauce)
- 1–2 green chillies (for that kick)
- 1 tsp cumin seeds (for the soul)
- 2 tbsp sour, thick curd (the thicker, the creamier)
- Salt, to taste, obviously
- A small chunk of jaggery (for a sweet surprise)
- ¼ tsp fenugreek seeds (a pinch of magic)
- 3–4 dried red chillies (to spice things up)
- 1 tsp rai (for the pop)
- A sprig of curry leaves (because they're the charmers)

- 1/4 tsp urad dal (for the crunch)
- A pinch of asafoetida

Method

1. Start by peeling and chopping those ripe mangoes into generous pieces. Add a pinch of turmeric powder and cook them in just a dash of water until they're halfway done. If you're feeling adventurous and have small mangoes, toss the whole thing in—yes, whole mangoes, and double down on that mango madness.
2. Grind together your freshly grated coconut, green chillies, and ginger to form a smooth

paste. This magical paste is your personal flavour bomb.

3. Pour your flavour-packed paste into the cooked mangoes. Add salt and a chunk of jaggery (adjust to your sweet tooth). Let this cook until it smells like heaven.
4. Once it's all done, switch off the flame and add your beautifully whisked sour curd (full-fat is the key for that luxurious creaminess). Do not, I repeat, *do not* heat it—let the residual heat work its magic.
5. Now comes the grand finale. For the tempering, heat up some coconut oil (don't skimp, we want this dish to shine) and toss in the rai, urad dal, dried red chillies, fenugreek, cumin seeds and curry leaves for that extra 'oomph'.
6. Serve it with love (and maybe a little extra rice because, well, this is a dish you can't get enough of).

Pro Tip

Pair with some crispy appalam and you'll be in flavour heaven faster than you can say 'nirvana'.

Salaaad: Always Said with Extra Flair

In my Sindhi home, no meal—whether it was a grand affair with guests or just the regular 'let's-feed-the-family' hustle—was ever complete without a plate of salad. And when I say salad, I mean a generously piled plate, like a vegetable fiesta waiting to happen. We're talking tomatoes, onions, cucumber, carrot, and of course, the ultimate showstopper—boiled beetroot. A sprinkle of salt, a dash of pepper, and a squeeze of lime to make everything look even fancier.

And guess what? This salad wasn't just for the pre-meal decorative parade—it was a mainstay at both lunch and dinner. Beetroot was treated like royalty—boiled, peeled, and sliced into thin rounds, served on a separate plate so that its vibrant red hue didn't cause any drama by mixing with the other veggies. The result? A plate full of rainbow veggies, each with a distinct personality.

Onions and tomatoes were the originals—no questions asked. Cucumber, however, had its restrictions (because, as in life, we must have boundaries). Not at night. Not in winter. The cucumber had rules, you see. And when radish was in season, it sauntered in, making everything look even more celebration-worthy.

But the cherry on top? The green chillies. Oh yes, a couple of fiery green chillies, sprinkled with a hefty heap of salt and a slice of lime on the side, made a dramatic entrance, as if to say, 'We're here to spice things up.'

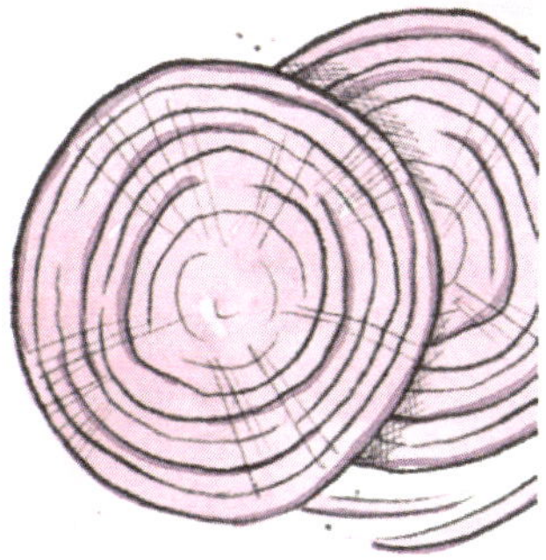

And then there was the raw mango—a seasonal diva, making a grand appearance in slices, fresh from the market, right onto the salad plate, especially at the mango season premiere.

But wait, there's more. This salad wasn't just an appetizer; it was part of the whole meal experience. We'd eat it between courses, with the meal and sometimes, just to finish off the plate. Leftovers? *Pfft*. Never heard of it. The salad always disappeared the fastest.

Now, let's pivot to my Tamilian roots. Onions? They were as elusive as a unicorn in my house. One chopped onion would last a week, making cameo appearances in upma, *poha* or a mixed vegetable sambar—always in the most modest of roles. The rare, special guest was the Madras onion, the rockstar that made its way into an exclusive sambar. And trust me, when it did, you treasured it.

Raw onions? In my Tamilian home, that was like a forbidden fruit. The only time raw onion made an appearance was very occasionally in a thogayal or a thayir *pachchadi*—a South Indian version of raita that includes ground coconut and a tempering of rai, urad dal and curry leaves.

So, yes, while Sindhi households treated salad like an all-star performer, in my Tamilian home, it was more like a subtle supporting character—never too flashy, never too much. Just enough to balance things out... and not rock the boat.

Pickled and Tickled

Ah, pickles—the one thing both my Sindhi and Tamilian households agreed on. Or rather, fought over. In the Sindhi corner, we had *khatain* (with a 'k' for *kick*), and in the Tamil corner, it was *oorugai*. And both the mothers treated pickles like top-secret recipes, passed down through generations… or so they claimed during their season-long discussions on what could and couldn't be pickled.

It always started the same way: small bowls of pickles exchanged like precious treasure—each bite weighed and scrutinised like it was an episode of 'MasterChef.' The moment one of these tiny bowls received approval, the signal was given: Large jars were coming. Oh yes, the jars. Because what's a pickle without a jar?

Now, Sindhi pickles were a whole vibe—especially the zero oil variety. Oil was an outsider in Mamma's pickle world. Her khatain was made in mustard water (ground mustard mixed with water), which I'm sure was invented just to give the yellow (sarson) mustard seeds a place to shine. Some pickles would take a turn into the 'fancy' world of *surko* (Sindhi for vinegar). But honestly, the basar (onion) khatain was the star. Simple, quick and oh-so-delicious, Mamma would whip up a batch, finish it off in record time, and declare, 'Done! On to the next one!' It was always made in small batches because, well, if pickles lasted too long, the interest in them waned slowly.

Meanwhile, in the Tamil household, oorugai was the sacred elixir. Each jar was treated like it was the last thing that would keep us alive through a world war. My Amma would go overboard with rai, fenugreek, and the occasional 'secret' ingredient that she only whispered to the pickle. And, of course, there were strict rules about when it could be eaten—right after you've eaten enough rice, and only if you've earned the privilege of having your taste buds assaulted with that glorious tang.

Both mothers, armed with their secret pickle weapons, would meet in the kitchen and swap jars like they were trading stocks on the pickled commodities market. Pickle inflation was real. If a jar didn't pass the taste test, there was always a polite exchange of 'maybe next time' while both sides secretly rolled their eyes and thought— 'this is so NOT going to share space on my shelves.'

In the end, pickles were more than just a condiment—they were a cultural exchange, a social contract, and a sacred ritual.

Paaniwaro Basar Khatain: Onion and Ground Mustard Mixed with Water

Ingredients

- 500 gm baby onions (picked with the precision of a diamond cutter by Mamma herself)
- Fresh garlic with green stalks (or simply 2–3 garlic cloves, if you want to be boring)
- ½ tsp red chilli powder (for that kick that'll leave you questioning your life choices)
- 1 tsp turmeric (because it's yellow and magical)
- Salt, to taste (trust Mamma, it's the perfect amount, just like the pickle)
- 1 tbsp yellow mustard seeds (roughly pounded to release their spicy secrets)
- Boiled and cooled water

Method

1. Slit the baby onions with the kind of precision that would make a surgeon proud, forming a '+' sign (it's all about that symmetry).
2. Wash and rinse the onions like you're giving them a spa day—thoroughly, of course.
3. Find an air-tight jar (because, you know, this pickle's important) and place the onions inside.
4. Add turmeric, chilli powder and salt—not just any salt, but the salt that will make you think you've discovered the meaning of life.
5. Roughly pound the yellow mustard seeds. Don't go overboard—this isn't a smoothie.

Just pound enough to release their bold flavours. Drop them in the jar.

6. Finely chop the garlic along with the stalks (because garlic with stalks is just more authentic), or chop the regular garlic cloves if you've decided to skip the drama.
7. Add the boiled and cooled water, covering the onions by an inch or two. Think of this as creating a pickle bath—no one likes a dry pickle.
8. Shake well, like you're auditioning for a pickle commercial.
9. Leave this jar in the sun for 2 days—because even pickles need a little sun therapy.
10. Lo and behold! Your pickle is ready to rock your taste buds.

Pro Tip

Since there's no oil to preserve it, this batch won't last forever. So, make it in small batches, unless you're planning on living with the consequences of a quick pickle demise.

And remember, Mamma didn't just stop at onions—carrot and turnip (aka *ghogrun*) were also her pickle victims. Every vegetable had its turn in the sun… literally.

Mango Madness in the Making: Amma's Pickle Alert

Step into Amma's home, and you're greeted by a heavenly whiff of raw mango—nature's way of announcing that mango season is just around the corner. The unmistakable tang in the air is your cue: something delicious is brewing in the kitchen.

Amma's just back from her favourite vegetable market, armed with her treasure—perfectly uniform baby mangoes, each handpicked with the precision of a jeweller inspecting diamonds. Why? To transform them into her legendary, lip-smacking pickle.

The countdown to mango mania has officially begun and trust me, it's going to be tangy, spicy and oh-so-irresistible.

Vadu Mangai: The Mango That Turns You into a Pickle Prodigy

Ingredients

- 2 cups of vadu mangai (maavadu or baby mangoes—they should be the round variety, because let's face it, perfectly round mangoes are a thing of beauty)
- 2–3 tbsp salt (rock salt preferred, because your taste buds deserve the royal treatment)
- 2 tbsp castor oil or sesame oil (choose your oil weapon wisely)

To Roast and Grind

- 20 dried red long chillies (medium spice—we're not trying to set your mouth on fire, just warm it up a bit)
- ½ tsp fenugreek seeds (because it's just a little bit bitter and a whole lot of awesome)
- ¾ tsp rai (don't skimp on the rai—it's the rai, baby)
- Small piece of turmeric (or ¼ tsp turmeric powder—the gold standard of spices)
- ¼ tsp asafoetida (the magical powder of flavour)

Method

1. First, select fresh baby mangoes. These little guys should be of a roughly same size and round enough to make you believe in perfection.
2. Wash them thoroughly and remove any stalks (unless you enjoy a bit of twine with your pickle).
3. Pat them dry like you're giving them a spa treatment—then shade dry to ensure no trace of water remains.
4. Transfer these babies into a porcelain bowl or a glass jar, one large enough to hold your mango army. Now pour in that oil—the more, the better.
5. Mix the oil through, like you're giving these mangoes their VIP treatment. They need to be coated, not shy.
6. Meanwhile, roast the spices:
   - Start with the chillies and add the fenugreek, rai and a dash of asafoetida (add

the asafoetida towards the end to get the maximum pungency).

- Turmeric? Don't roast it. It stays pure and golden.

7. Roast until the rai starts cracking—keep the flame on medium, or you'll end up with smoke signals instead of spices.
8. Let the roasted mixture cool down. Once it's cool, grind everything with salt into a smooth paste.
9. Add ¼ cup of boiled and cooled water to the ground spice mix. This is where the magic happens.
10. Now, pour the spicy paste over the mangoes and give them a good mix. Alternatively, seal the jar and shake it like you're shaking off your responsibilities.
11. Toss the jar 3–4 times a day to ensure the spices make their way into every nook and cranny of the mangoes. In the first few days, the mangoes will shrink as the salt gets to work, making them oozier and saucier by the day.
12. In 2 days, you'll see the magic beginning, but it'll take at least a week for them to reach their full, pickled glory.

Pro Tip

Amma would always make a huge batch at the start of mango season, filling up a big jar. This jar would eventually end up in Mamma's kitchen, where Mamma loved to enjoy it. Her favourite way? Bite into a whole mango, then pour a spoonful of that tangy, spicy, red gravy over hot rice, mix it in and voilà—divine. Because why eat normal food when you can eat like royalty?

Enjoy, pickle lovers.

When They Weren't Cooking

Amma's afternoons were a sacred retreat into the world of words. You could always find her nestled comfortably between the covers of Tamil magazines like *Ananda Vikatan*, *Kalki*, or *Amudhasurabi*. Her mind would wander to faraway places and intriguing stories—Jayakantan, Shivasankari, or Sujata were her regular companions. But if she was in the mood for something extra special, she'd reach for

the magical pages of Ruskin Bond, letting his tales from the mountains whisk her away. On those rare, inspired afternoons, Amma would pull out her notebook and pen. With every stroke, the Tamil script would dance, each letter elegantly curving, creating a rhythm of its own. Her handwriting had a unique tilt to it—just like her thoughts—filling pages with a quiet kind of beauty.

Now, in my other home, across the landing, was Mamma, who transformed the mundane into something extraordinary. There she was, diligently pedalling away at her old sewing machine—a machine almost as ancient as her arrival in India. Her bed would often resemble a patchwork quilt of sorts, covered in scraps of fabric of all shapes and sizes. Scissors in hand, Mamma could weave magic into the most unexpected pieces. Leftover fabric? Oh, that was never discarded. Much like the way she could work wonders with food, Mamma transformed these scraps into covers of every conceivable kind. Whether it was a mixer cover, TV cover, sofa cover, or cushion cover, nothing was too small to be repurposed. And, as always, a delicate string of lace would adorn the edges—giving each piece its own little makeover. Roti covers? You bet. Anything that needed a cover or could use a little TLC, Mamma was ready to give it a new lease of life. There was a beautiful practicality to her and in her hands, even the leftovers told a story—a story of creativity, sustainability, and love. And so, in their own ways, both Amma and Mamma created worlds. One with words, the other with thread—but both filled with warmth, wisdom, and a whole lot of heart.

Food for the Gods

Both Amma and Mamma were devout in their own quirky ways and I've happily adopted a mix of both.

Every now and then, Mamma would get in one of her solemn moods and decide it was time for a Satyanarayan puja at home. The kind of mood where she was channelling all her inner goddess energy. On the morning of the puja, she'd surprise the whole household (which was basically my husband, son, and myself) by waking up before dawn—a huge deal for someone whose relationship with the sun was... let's say, complicated. The sun and Mamma only agreed on two things: airing out mattresses in the sun and letting freshly pickled veggies soak up some rays.

But on puja day? Mamma was a changed woman. She was bathed, dressed, and had a look on her face like she was preparing to light up the heavens with her devotion. And, of course, she claimed the kitchen. Now, Mamma was all of 4'7" on a good day, so to ensure she could reach the gas stove and cook like a pro, she had a footstool made of sheesham (Indian rosewood) wood—her trusty sidekick. This was no ordinary stool. It was her throne, her platform to greatness. I remember when we moved to a new house years later, I got the kitchen platform built lower, but that stool remained... waiting for its next adventure.

On puja day, Mamma would drape a chiffon dupatta over her head and bow humbly to the stove. She would raise herself to full height and get started to whip up food for the gods (and us, of course). The prasad she made was always simple yet divine: *kutti* prasad—a grainy, delicious little number with wheat flour, sugar, peanuts, and oil. Sometimes I think the gods themselves were envious of our prasad.

Meanwhile, across the lobby at Amma's house, the routine was a bit more predictable. For Amma, Thursdays, Fridays and Saturdays were special—she'd prepare an offering for the Lord on these days. The choices? Sakkarai pongal, panchamrutham or *kesari*. No exceptions, just a rotating menu of divine offerings. On these days, Amma would still rise early (because, well, that's her thing), but she'd linger a bit longer at the altar, chanting with more fervour than usual, eyes closed, devotion flowing like ghee.

Amma's kesari was legendary in my Sindhi home. We'd always get a generous helping after the prayer rituals. Simple, sweet, and filled with love. Semolina, sugar, ghee, topped with dry fruits, green cardamom and sometimes even a hint of edible camphor. But over time, I decided to make a few modifications—you know, out of convenience and just a slight personal touch.

We started doing the Satyanarayan puja monthly and instead of just pure kesari or kutti, I created a hybrid version—*sheera* (my way). No saffron for me; I wanted it to resemble the simple, humble kutti but with a smoother, creamier texture like that of the kesari. Plus, the dry kutti always managed to stick to the roof of my mouth, so I figured why not make it a bit more user-friendly? The gods would understand... I hope.

Satsangs and Bhajanais

Both sets of parents were, let's just say, devout—and they took their satsangs and bhajanais very seriously.

My Tamilian parents, true to form, returned from every bhajanai looking like they'd been to a monastery. They came back with solemn gifts—fruit, kesari or sakkarai pongal, as if they were bringing home a divine treasure. 'Eat this prasad,' Amma would say, 'It's the essence of purity!' I never questioned it. I just ate it, and said, 'Thanks,' to the gods.

Mamma, on the other hand, took a very different approach to satsangs. She would return from her Sindhi–Punjabi community satsang with bags full of gourmet prasad—think samosas, tikki chhole, gulab jamun... The woman was practically a walking buffet when she arrived home. The moment she entered the house; it was like the gates of heaven had opened—samosas and chai for everyone. So much for spiritual enlightenment; we were all too busy stuffing our faces to worry about our karma.

And then, a truly memorable chapter in our lives began. My husband and I—reluctantly—found ourselves hosting two satsangs at our house, both at the insistent pleas of our parents. Because apparently, the universe didn't need just one satsang; it needed TWO. So, we hosted one for each side.

First up, the Iyer bhajanai—and let's just say, this was not your casual, laid-back affair. Oh no. This was a military operation disguised as a spiritual gathering. The men and women arrived at the exact minute, sat in perfect alignment, and gave side-eye to anyone who even whispered. I swear, if you sneezed, you'd be excommunicated from the room. And once the singing was over, everyone left with—wait for it—bananas and kesari. That's right. Bananas.

Then came Mamma's satsang. Now, Mamma's satsang? Oh, it was an experience—and by 'experience,' I mean a spiritual scavenger hunt. The women arrived, give or take 15 minutes from the announced start time. Punctuality was clearly optional, but the key was that when the ladies showed up, it was like a reunion of old friends who hadn't seen each other in years. First things first: the official tour of the house. A must. If you weren't led through the house by Mamma herself, did you even attend the satsang? Then came the first round of tea and biscuits. I know, right? Who needs enlightenment when you have tea and biscuits?

Now, let's talk about *monita*—which, by the way, isn't a person, it's a Sindhi delight served to guests. Think of it as an upgraded canapé, topped with boiled and mashed potato, finely chopped onions and tomatoes. It was served with a side of jalebi and mini vada pav, because why not? We also added yet another round of tea and biscuits. You could tell the latecomers were a little upset about missing the house tour, but Mamma was always there to save the day. No one missed out on the full Mamma experience—whether they arrived on time or not.

And that's how we learned: Satsang at Mamma's house didn't just nourish the soul; they nourished the body too—one canapé at a time.

Gyarasi Dhodho Bhaji: Ekadashi Feast, Mamma Style

Mamma was all about tradition, and when it came to ekadashi, she wasn't just fasting—she was cooking up magic. On this day, she would avoid any grains and instead, make a thick, golden flatbread (yes, *dhodho*) that had the magical power to make your taste buds do a happy dance. And as a sidekick? Oh, the *gyarasi* bhaji made with lotus stem and potato. This was a meal that could make the heavens pause for a second to enjoy the aroma.

Now, if I was in my room and heard Mamma ask for a plain white sheet of paper, I just knew what was coming. Dhodho. It couldn't be made with a rolling pin—no, no, no. It had to be delicately patted on a sheet of paper sprinkled with flour, like she was crafting an edible masterpiece. There was no rolling this dough, only love and careful hand patting.

And even though Mamma was the one fasting, we were all forced into an involuntary fast too because no one else was allowed to cook anything else. The anticipation. The waiting. The hungry stares. But trust me, it was worth it. It's a dish so delicious that I could eat it every day. Every. Single. Day.

Here's how Mamma made these dishes that could tempt even the gods:

(Makes 4)

Ingredients

- 3 cups sauri atta (bhagar flour or varia)
- 2 boiled and mashed potatoes
- Salt, to taste
- A pinch of freshly ground pepper
- 1 tbsp cooking oil

Method

1. Mix all ingredients into a dough by slowly adding water. The dough should be soft, like a cloud, but firm enough to pat out into a roti.
2. Divide the dough into 4 portions.
3. Take each portion, place it on a sheet of paper (and sprinkle it with flour so it doesn't stick) and gently pat it into a round shape. Think of it as the dough equivalent of a slow dance.
4. Heat a tawa and grease it with a drop of oil. Gently lift the paper and flip the roti onto the tawa, peeling away the sheet of paper with the grace of a pro.
5. Cook both sides on medium flame, applying a spoonful of oil on each side for that golden crispiness.
6. When it's perfectly golden, serve hot with the gyarasi bhaji.

Gyarasi Beeh Aloo Bhaji: With Salt and Pepper, Just like Mamma Did

(Serves 3)

Ingredients

- 1 or 2 potatoes
- 1 lotus stem (sliced diagonally)
- 1 tbsp sauri atta (bhagar flour or varia)
- Salt, to taste
- Freshly ground pepper
- 1 tbsp aamchur or half a cup of tamarind pulp

Method

1. Boil the potato and lotus stem with a pinch of salt. Mamma always used a pressure cooker, because why wait? She was a woman on a mission.
2. Set aside to cool (and prepare for the next phase of your taste adventure).
3. Heat 1 tablespoon of oil in a pan. Then add 1 tablespoon of sauri atta (the same flour used for dhodho) and roast it, keeping an eye on it so it doesn't burn. Once it changes colour slightly, add a glass of water.
4. Stir, stir, stir. No lumps allowed.
5. Let it boil and thicken slightly and then add salt to taste (remember, the veggies already have salt).
6. Add a teaspoon of freshly ground pepper and let the mixture simmer.
7. Add the boiled potatoes and lotus stem to the pan and give everything a good mix.
8. Add a little more water (about half a glass) to adjust the consistency.
9. Sprinkle in the aamchur powder or tamarind pulp for that tangy punch—and don't be shy, the tangier, the better.
10. Cover and bring it to a boil. Boom. Bhaji is ready.

Alternate Method

Sometimes Mamma would make this in the pressure cooker. Same steps, but no need to pre-boil the veggies. Just toss everything into the cooker, 3 whistles and 5 minutes on simmer, and voilà! The magic happens.

Once it was all ready, we gathered around the table and let me tell you, this was not just a meal. It was a spiritual experience, one that made you appreciate every grain of the dhodho and every burst of flavour from the bhaji.

Ammavasai Day: Seriousness Meets Sizzle

Ah, ammavasai—the day when seriousness hung in the air like an unwanted guest who never left. The calm before the culinary storm that was about to erupt in Amma's kitchen. While Appa, in his usual 'let's do this quickly and quietly' mode, would rush through his *tarpanam* ritual, Amma was already in full kitchen battle mode, orchestrating a meal that would make even a king go, 'Who needs a throne when you have this food?'

Appa's job was simple: get up early, bathe (no, not a luxury shower, just a quick dip) and then spend an hour in wet clothes, surrounded by *dharbhai* grass and silverware. He'd mutter incantations while holding various shiny utensils, his focus so intense that we'd sometimes wonder if he was in the middle of a secret magic ritual or simply trying to locate the right utensil.

Meanwhile, Amma, the true heroine of the day, was holding down the fort in the kitchen, sweating it out like a gladiator prepping for battle. She had an array of tasks lined up for us, all of which would require our utmost concentration and perfect execution (according to her, of course). We were in the kitchen, running random errands like grating coconuts, frying pappadams, and stirring the payasam—the kind of tasks that made us feel like we were part of a royal kitchen crew. Except there were no aprons—only a steady stream of 'Hurry up!' and 'Focus!' echoing through the kitchen.

Once Appa completed his ritual (which involved copious amounts of water, sesame seeds and dharbhai grass that was apparently as holy as the water), we'd rush to clean up, lay out the banana leaves and transform our living room into what can only be described as a spiritual food feast. And mind you, nothing with onion, garlic, drumstick or potatoes would make its way onto the leaf. That was the real spiritual deal: a hearty meal without the usual suspects.

Now, let's talk about what's *actually* required for a tarpanam ritual, in case you're ever invited to perform one (or just curious):

1. Water: The primary ingredient, as it turns out, isn't some exotic herb or mystical flower. Nope. Just good ol' water. A lot of it.
2. Sesame Seeds: The humble sesame seeds, also known as 'ellu' or 'til' (fancy, right?), are the unsung heroes of this ritual.

3. Dharbhai: Holy grass. Yes, grass. But not just any grass—dharbhai. Apparently, it's pure enough to purify even your most stubborn thoughts. Who knew grass had such power?

As for the tarpanam days? Well, they're performed on days when the universe tells you it's time for a little spiritual cleanse, like *aadi* ammavasai, *mahalaya* ammavasai and *thai* ammavasai. These are the days when you'd find Appa wrapped in sacred seriousness, Amma transforming into the head chef of the year and my sister, my brother and I… well, we were just there for the food.

And when that meal was finally served? Trust me, the joy was pure and simple—because if you had Amma's cooking on a serious, sacred day like ammavasai, you knew that you were in the presence of greatness.

Healing Recipes: The Ultimate Soul Food

Every couple of months, Amma would declare a 'Spartan Day'—a day for a frugal meal that, to the untrained eye, might look simple but was actually a ticket to flavour heaven. Picture this: paruppu podi (dal powder), *milagu* kuzhambu (pepper gravy), steamed rice, and *vazhakkai* upperi (raw banana stir-fry) served with all the warmth of a hug and a side of soul-cleansing vibes.

And Amma's explanation? Oh, she'd just casually say, 'To cleanse the system,' like it was the most obvious thing in the world. Well, let's be honest, no one needed an explanation when you're about to eat a meal like that. Only an idiot would turn their nose up at it.

The steaming hot rice was the star of the show, with each grain soft and fluffy, just waiting to be kissed by a scoop of paruppu podi and a generous glug of homemade ghee—the kind that has the power to transport you to a place of pure bliss. The warmth of it all, the richness of the ghee, the simplicity of the flavours… it was like a spiritual experience for your taste buds.

Now, let's talk about the vazhakkai upperi, the humble hero of this dish. The raw banana gets sliced and lovingly tossed in a pan, sizzling away with rai, curry leaves and a delicate balance of spices. It's crispy, it's tender, and oh, it pairs perfectly with that rice and kuzhambu like they were meant to be together since the beginning of time.

Amma, with her ever-practical approach to health and wellness, whipped up this spread of dishes designed not just to nourish, but to cleanse and revitalise the body from within. Each dish was a mix of simple yet potent ingredients that did more than fill the stomach—they replenished the soul. Every dish served as both a remedy and a celebration. The focus was on earthy flavours and wholesome textures, often using spices and herbs known for their restorative powers.

For Amma, these dishes weren't just about feeding the family; they were about ensuring that every bite served a greater purpose: healing, balancing and nourishing, each ingredient chosen for its rich medicinal benefits. Her approach to cooking was instinctive and ritualistic, like an old family secret passed down through generations. Whether it was a chilly winter day or a rainy afternoon, Amma knew how to whip up a dish that would not only warm your body but also bring peace and clarity to your mind. And the best part? You never realised you were being healed because you were too busy enjoying the flavours.

Vazhakkai Upperi: A Kerala Delight

Why Kerala? Well, we hail from Palakkad that literally sits on the fence between Tamil Nadu and Kerala. Our social mores and culinary patterns are thus, a mix of both the lands.

If you've ever had the pleasure of sitting down to a traditional Kerala feast, then you know there's always that one side dish that steals the show. For me, it's the heavenly vazhakkai (raw banana). This veggie has this gorgeous texture that makes it so satisfying to eat. There's something about it that feels hearty and grounding—yet still light enough to pair perfectly with a bowl of steaming rice. The mix of coconut, turmeric, and the unmistakable flavour of coconut oil takes this dish from delicious to addictive.

And let's not even talk about the absolute joy of scraping the last bits off the vessel after the dish is finished. Trust me, that coconut-starch crust that's formed at the bottom is like a prize. But enough of my rambling—let's get down to the recipe. This one's bound to transport you straight to the backwaters of Kerala.

(Serves 3)

Ingredients

- 4 or 5 vazhakkai, peeled and cubed
- ½ tsp turmeric powder, and a bit of salt
- ¾ cup grated coconut (fresh or desiccated)
- 3 green chillies, chopped
- A pinch of cumin

For Tempering

- Coconut oil (for that authentic flavour)
- 2 dried red chillies
- ½ tsp rai
- A sprig of curry leaves
- Salt, to taste

Method

1. Place the vazhakkai cubes into a pot with salt, turmeric and about two-and-a-half cups of water. Bring it to a boil and let it simmer until the banana is tender and the water is almost dried up—leaving behind a bit of moisture but not a pool of water.
2. While the vazhakkai is cooking, take your grated coconut, green chillies, cumin and crush them together in a mortar and pestle until you have a coarse paste. If you're feeling lazy (and who isn't?), you can give it a few pulses in the electric mixer to save time.
3. Once the vazhakkai is cooked and the water has evaporated, create a little well in the centre of the pot. Add the freshly made coconut paste into this well. Gently cover the mix with a lid and let it simmer on a low flame for about 5–7 minutes. This helps the flavours meld together. If it looks like the mix is sticking to the bottom, don't panic—just add a bit of hot water to loosen it up and mix it well.
4. In a separate pan, heat some coconut oil (because, let's face it, nothing beats the flavour of coconut oil in Kerala cooking).

Add rai and let them crackle. Once that magic happens, add dried red chillies and curry leaves and fry them for a minute or two. The aroma will have you salivating—guaranteed.

5. Pour this tempering over the vazhakkai and coconut mixture, stirring gently to combine all the flavours. Add salt to taste and let it simmer for a few more minutes to ensure everything is infused with those aromatic spices.
6. Once the dish is cooked to perfection, serve it hot with a bowl of steamed rice. Trust me, there's no better way to enjoy this than with a steaming plate of rice and a generous drizzle of coconut oil on top.

Pro Tip

Sometimes, Amma would add peeled and cubed *suran* (elephant foot yam) along with the vazhakkai. Just made it more earthy and hearty.

So go ahead, indulge in this Kerala-style vazhakkai upperi and let your taste buds embark on a flavourful journey. You might just find yourself scraping the vessel for the last bit—don't worry, I won't judge.

Paruppu Podi: The Ultimate Comfort in a Spoon

Let's talk about paruppu podi, that magical dal powder that can turn even the laziest of days into a cozy, satisfying meal. When mixed with hot, steaming rice and a dollop of ghee, it's like the universe decided to give you a hug in the form of food. This recipe is a lifesaver when you're craving something hearty yet simple and the best part? You probably have all the ingredients lying around, just waiting to be transformed into a delicious meal.

Paruppu podi comes in many versions, but this is the tried and tested one that's been perfected in my home. The dal-based powder is like the Swiss Army knife of Tamilian kitchens—super versatile, simple to make and oh-so-delicious. Just mix it into white rice, throw in some ghee or oil, and voilà—instant satisfaction. And when you add a crispy, crunchy appalam to the mix, well, let's just say you're living the dream.

Shelf life is almost a month if refrigerated, so get started. Here is how you make it:

(Serves 4)

Ingredients

- ½ cup tuvar dal
- ½ cup yellow moong dal
- ½ cup urad dal
- 1 tsp whole black peppercorns
- 1 tsp cumin seeds
- 4 dried red chillies
- ¼ tsp asafoetida
- Salt, to taste
- 1 tsp sesame oil

Method

1. Heat a pan and dry roast all the dal separately until they turn a lovely golden brown. When roasting the moong dal, add the red chillies.
2. Set the roasted dal aside. This is where the magic begins—those roasted dal flavours are going to be next-level.
3. In the same pan, add oil. Drop in the whole black peppercorns and fry it for just 30 seconds. Then add the cumin seeds, and give them a quick fry. Trust me, that smoky aroma is your signal that things are about to get really good.
4. Toss in the salt and the asafoetida, mix it with the roasted dal and spices, and let everything cool off.

5. Once everything is cool, throw it into a mixer and grind it all into a fine powder. That's your paruppu podi ready to go.

Paruppu podi used to be a constant staple in Amma's kitchen because, let's be honest, who doesn't love a meal that's equal parts comforting, nutritious and ridiculously easy to make? As I write this, I am ruing the fact that I have been postponing the making of this super podi.

Milagu Kuzhambu: A Cozy Hug in a Bowl

There's something about milagu kuzhambu that instantly transports you to the comfort of home, especially on those rainy days or when the sniffles hit. The spicy warmth of black pepper paired with the tanginess of tamarind—this kuzhambu is the definition of soul food. It's a perfect remedy for the cold and let's be real, a surefire way to chase away any sniffles or chills.

This traditional Tamil kuzhambu is a pepper-packed powerhouse. It's got that unmistakable peppery kick that makes you sit up straight (and reach for more rice). Best part? It's super simple to whip up and has an incredibly long shelf life, making it the kind of dish you can prepare in bulk and keep for up to two weeks. Ghee or *gingelly* (sesame) oil and a dollop of this spicy-tangy milagu kuzhambu with a side of crispy appalam, is a meal that feels like a warm blanket on a chilly day.

(Serves 3)

Ingredients

- 1½ tsp whole black peppercorns
- 2 tsp urad dal
- 2 tsp chana dal
- 2 tsp coriander seeds
- 2–3 dried red chillies (for extra heat)
- A few curry leaves
- A pinch of asafoetida
- 1 big lemon-sized tamarind ball (soaked and pulped)
- Salt, to taste
- 1 tbsp gingelly oil (or any cooking oil)
- 1 tsp rai
- 1 tsp jaggery powder (Amma's addition, optional, for a hint of sweetness)

Method

1. In a bowl, dissolve the tamarind pulp in water (about a cup) and set it aside. If you're using a block of tamarind, soak it in warm water and extract the pulp.
2. Prep the pepper paste. Heat ½ teaspoon of oil in a skillet. Drop in the red chillies first. When they begin to turn brown, add the whole black peppercorns, the urad dal, the chana dal, the coriander seeds and asafoetida. Fry on medium flame. The burst of peppery flavour is what makes this dish stand out, so don't skimp on this step. Add the curry leaves at the end. Remove and let it cool.
3. Transfer to the grinder and grind to a smooth paste, adding water little by little. The consistency is key—smooth but not watery.
4. In a pan, heat the gingelly oil. Once hot, add rai. Let them splutter and sizzle for a few seconds. Then, add the curry leaves and fry for another 30 seconds until fragrant. Then add a pinch of asafoetida.
5. Now, pour in the tamarind water. Add salt to taste and let the whole thing boil until the sharp tangy aroma of tamarind vanishes.
6. Now, the ground paste makes it grand entry—add it to the tamarind water. Stir well to avoid lumps. Add the jaggery.
7. Bring the mixture to a boil and let it simmer for about 10–15 minutes or until it thickens and the flavours meld together. The longer it simmers, the better it tastes.
8. Once it's thickened to your liking, take it off the heat. Serve it piping hot with steamed white rice and a spoonful of ghee.

Why We Love It

- Pepper Power: This dish is a powerhouse of peppery goodness, perfect for those days when you need a little extra warmth.
- Long Shelf Life: It can be stored in the fridge for up to two weeks. So, if you're making it in bulk, you're set for a while.
- Comfort Food: There's nothing like sitting down to a plate of rice with milagu kuzhambu and if it's raining outside, all the better.

Perfect for the rainy season or any time you feel under the weather, this dish is as much about tradition as it is about the comfort of home. Simple, spicy, tangy and oh-so-delicious, milagu kuzhambu is guaranteed to warm you up from the inside out.

The Simplicity of Halko Khaado

Sindhi healing foods that Mamma made were a beautiful contrast to the rich and spiced dishes she usually prepared. There were days when she embraced *halko khaado*, which meant simplicity—a little less spice, a little less oil, almost bordering on bland. It wasn't that she wasn't fond of her usual bold flavours, but there was something soothing in these moments of frugality. On such days, she would always add a generous dollop of curd into her dishes—its cool, creamy texture balancing the taste.

Mamma's absolute favourite during these days was *bhath*—a dish made with broken wheat instead of rice. The broken wheat was a hearty and wholesome alternative, providing a grounding, earthy flavour that felt like a perfect antidote to a busy day. She would make a big pot of it, knowing that her grandson would always be excited to join her at the table. The two of them, sitting side by side, would dive into the bowl, savouring each bite as though it held memories of laughter and love. The bhath wasn't just a dish; it was a moment of connection, a small ritual where flavours and affection met. It was a meal that spoke of warmth, simplicity and the timeless bond of family—quiet yet powerful in its healing.

Amma, too, loved the bhath. It had the same comforting, sweet taste as the paruppu payasam she often made for the gods on auspicious days. The textures of both the dishes were so alike, and Mamma, too, had always adored the payasam.

One morning, Mamma's frail voice echoed from the living room: 'Make your Mummy's bhath.' Her words, though soft, held a quiet yearning. I instantly knew what she was asking for and as I began preparing it, I could feel a wave of nostalgia wash over me. But something felt incomplete.

I crossed the lobby to Amma, passing on Mamma's request to her. Without a word, Amma's eyes brightened and within the hour, she returned with a large bowl of steaming paruppu payasam, the very dish that had bonded them over the years. But she didn't leave it on the table. No, Amma was meticulous in her care—she walked to Mamma's room, where Mamma sat propped up on her bed, listening to spiritual songs on her old radio.

Amma entered with the bowl, her frail hands steady as she placed it gently before Mamma. Then, with a knowing smile, she asked me to pull up a chair by the bedside. And there they were—together. Amma, softly talking, sharing stories of old, while Mamma took delicate spoonfuls of 'my Mummy's bhath,' savouring each bite with a contented smile.

It wasn't just the food; it was the love that filled the room—the love of a daughter honouring her mother's traditions, and the love of a mother, still giving, still nurturing, even when her strength had long since started to fade. It was a moment I would carry with me forever, etched in my heart, as a reminder of how deeply love can be woven into the smallest acts.

Wholesome *Bhath*: Broken Wheat Porridge

A simple, nourishing dish that fills you with warmth and goodness. Here's how to make it:

(*Serves 3*)

Ingredients

I do know of some people who add green cardamom, coconut, nutmeg, and dry fruit. But Mamma kept it simple, always.

- 2 cups of lapsi (broken wheat)
- A ladle of any cooking oil (I later stealthily moved to ghee)
- 2 cups of jaggery powder
- 3 cups water
- A glass of milk

Method

1. Heat ghee in the cooker, add the broken wheat and sauté on high flame for 2 minutes. Then lower the heat and cook for 15–20 minutes, stirring occasionally until the wheat changes colour and releases a nice aroma.
2. Add 3 cups of water, stir and cover the cooker. Pressure cook for about 20 minutes.
3. Once you open the cooker, add jaggery powder and give it a good mix. Switch on the stove and let the mixture cook until the jaggery fully melts.
4. Add a glass of milk to the mixture and let the whole thing simmer for 5 minutes.

That's it. This is a perfect wholesome meal—comforting and packed with energy. Enjoy.

Paruppu Payasam: The Magical Delight

I make this delicious treat in the pressure cooker, thanks to my Sindhi lessons. Amma didn't—but this shortcut makes life a little sweeter. Amma always used to melt the jaggery and strain out every little impurity before adding it to the milk and dal. Let's get started.

(Serves 3)

Ingredients

- ½ cup *pasi* paruppu (yellow moong dal) and a clutch of chana dal for that extra bite
- ¼ cup jaggery (adjust to your sweet tooth's liking)
- ½ cup milk (oh, the creamy goodness)
- Water (a little splash, just to balance things out)
- 1 tsp ghee (because everything's better with ghee)
- 1 green cardamom, powdered (for that fragrant magic)
- A handful of raisins and 4 cashews, broken into pieces (for a crunchy surprise)

Method

1. Start by roasting the moong dal with a little ghee until it gives off that lovely fragrance. Add the chana dal. But hey, don't let them get too brown—we want just a hint of that nutty aroma.
2. Add about ¾ cup of water and the milk to the dal and pressure cook for up to 3 whistles. Your kitchen will smell like a dream.
3. Once the pressure's done its thing, open it up and give the dal a nice mash-up. Add your powdered jaggery and stir it all together, letting that sweetness melt right in. Or, you could melt the jaggery separately, strain it, and then add it to the dal mixture.
4. Turn the heat down low and let it simmer for another 2 minutes. Need to adjust the consistency? Just add a little more milk or water, depending on how you like it.
5. Fry some raisins and cashew nuts in a bit of ghee, and add them to the payasam to take the flavour up a notch. Yum.
6. Sprinkle the cardamom powder and breathe in the aroma.
7. Here's the key: don't overcook or mash the dal too much. Texture is everything. Serve it warm.

You are ready to treat your taste buds to a bowl of comfort.

Mamma's Thadal: Summer's Best Friend

When the sun blazed in the peak of summer, Mamma would work her magic in the kitchen, whipping up a tall glass of *thadal*. This cooling, energising drink was Mamma's secret weapon against the heat. Plus, it was a personal favourite of the *pehelwans* (wrestlers) because, hey, who doesn't want to feel like a champ?

(Serves 4)

Ingredients

- 2 tbsp *char magaz* (melon seeds)
- 1 tbsp khus khus (poppy seeds)
- A handful of almonds
- A pinch of black pepper
- 1–2 tbsp sugar (adjust to taste)
- 2 cups chilled water
- A few ice-cubes

Method

1. In a blender, combine the melon seeds, poppy seeds, almonds and black pepper. Grind this goodness until you get a smooth paste.
2. Add the chilled water to the paste and blend again until well-mixed.
3. Add sugar and a few ice cubes to the mix, and blend for a refreshing, chilled and sweetened finish.
4. Pour the thadal into glasses and enjoy the cooling, energising sip that beats the heat.

With this drink, you're not just cooling down—you're recharging and feeling like a summer champion.

Mamma didn't just make thadal as a one-time summer refreshment. She turned it into a syrup to keep in the fridge for those scorching days when you needed an instant escape from the heat. She'd prepare a concentrated batch, storing it neatly in a bottle, and whenever the heat got too much, she'd simply add a spoonful of this cooling elixir into a glass of chilled water. One sip, and it felt like you were taking a dip in a cool, serene river—an instant refresher.

Phakki or *Faqi*: Your Tummy's Best Friend and Immunity Booster

This aromatic Sindhi energy booster was always stocked in Mamma's fridge. No sooner did the batch run low than a fresh one was on the way. Packed with flavours and nutrients, *phakki* is a magical powder you can munch on directly.

Ingredients

- 50 gm fennel seeds
- 50 gm whole black peppercorn
- 10 *jwar ji tikki* (peppermint candy)
- 1 tsp misri (rock sugar)
- 3 green cardamom pods
- 1 tsp cumin seeds
- 1 tsp poppy seeds
- 50 gm each of cashews, almonds, pistachios, walnuts and pitted dry dates

Method

1. Coarsely grind all the dry fruits, and then blend in the fennel seeds, cumin seeds, poppy seeds, black peppercorn, peppermint, rock sugar and cardamom pods together.
2. Stir everything together and store in an airtight container.

Take a spoonful, and follow it up with a glass of warm water. It's packed with energy and nutrition.

Sindhi Khichdi: A Bowl of Comfort, a Ladle of Love

There's a kind of magic in simple food. For our family, that magic was *Sindhi khichdi*—a humble, soul-soothing dish that found its way onto the dinner table once a week. Paired with jeera aloo and dahi, it was as spartan as a Sindhi meal could get, yet it carried a warmth that filled both stomachs and hearts.

Mamma made her khichdi with rice and *chilkewali hari* moong dal (split green moong dal). Back in my Tamilian household, this dal was almost a stranger. The idea of khichdi itself never quite entered Amma's kitchen, where pongal—with its rice and yellow moong—ruled the roost. And so, Mamma's khichdi stayed a memory, a quiet favourite that didn't make it past family lore.

But in recent months, life came full circle. As I searched for soft, light dinner options for my ageing parents—something gentle enough for Amma's missing teeth, something that wouldn't weigh heavy on their stomachs—I found myself reaching for Mamma's old recipe. I made it her way, every step a tribute: simple, wholesome, comforting.

The first time I served it, with fresh curd and a dollop of *elumichai* oorugai (tangy Tamil lemon pickle), I watched my parents take their first bites with a mix of hope and trepidation. To my delight, it was an instant hit. Since then, the request has been the same, every other night: 'Khichdi again, please.'

And as they relish each spoonful, I can't help but feel Mamma's presence. I imagine her smiling down on them, on me, on the enduring love that food can carry across generations.

Thank you, Mamma, for the simplest of dishes, and for reminding us that even the most unassuming bowl of khichdi can be a vessel for so much love.

Try it, you will touch hearts.

This isn't just a recipe; it's a warm hug in a bowl. Perfect for days when you want something hearty yet comforting, this Sindhi khichdi is simple to make and oh-so-satisfying. Pair it with curd, crispy potatoes, roasted papad or all three for the ultimate comfort meal.

Here's how you can whip it up:

(Serves 3)

Ingredients

- 1 cup rice
- ½ cup split green moong dal, washed and soaked together for 30 minutes
- 2 tsp cooking oil or ghee (what can be better than pure ghee?)
- Salt, to taste
- 1 tsp cumin powder

Method

1. Heat the ghee in a trusty pressure cooker. Let the aroma of warm ghee signal that something good is about to happen.
2. Add the soaked rice and dal to the cooker, letting them sizzle for a moment as they meet the oil.
3. Pour in 2 glasses of water—don't skimp, this is where the magic begins. Add salt to taste.
4. Close the cooker and let everything cook for 3 whistles. Then lower the heat, simmer, and let it cook for an extra 10 minutes (patience is the secret ingredient here).
5. Once the cooker cools down and you've opened the lid, it's time for the twist. Add a generous spoonful of ghee and sprinkle in the cumin powder. Mix it well, letting the flavours meld beautifully.
6. If you're like me and love your khichdi extra mushy, add a splash of boiling water to the mixture, and give it another good stir.

Serve it piping hot with a dollop of fresh curd on the side, crispy shallow-fried potatoes or crunchy roasted papad. Like I said earlier, better yet, treat yourself to all three—it's comfort food; no one's judging.

This hearty, creamy khichdi is not just a meal; it's a reminder of love, warmth and the joy of simple pleasures.

Where the 'Twains Almost Met

If there's one dish that came close to bridging the culinary gap between the two mothers, it would be the Sindhi kadhi and its almost-Tamilian counterpart, the sambar. Now at first glance, you might think these two dishes come from worlds apart—Sindhi kadhi, a tangy, slightly spiced concoction made from gram flour and the Tamilian sambar, a rich hearty delight made with tuvar dal. But upon deeper inspection, these two dishes share more similarities than you'd expect, almost as if the culinary 'twains were about to meet.

Both are served with rice, both boast a generous helping of vegetables, and both owe their tangy zest to tamarind juice. The consistency? Almost identical. Both dishes pack a punch of flavour, thanks to their spices and the magical concoction of dal and vegetables. The emotions they evoke are remarkably similar too—comfort, warmth, and a feeling of home. They're the kind of dishes that bring families together, making long, hectic days a little bit more bearable.

And then, of course, there's the humble potato. In Sindhi cuisine, you'll find aloo *tuk* paired with kadhi—a crispy, golden-fried potato that contrasts beautifully with the smooth, tangy kadhi. In Tamil kitchens, the aloo curry usually accompanies the sambar, its spicy, soft texture complementing the savoury flavours of the sambar. It's a marriage of the earthy potato with the flavourful gravies that ties both these iconic dishes together.

Though both the mothers adored these dishes, their loyalties were, of course, firmly rooted in their own traditions. Amma, being the quintessential Tamilian, would always show a special fondness for her sambar, lovingly ladling it over rice, while Mamma, with her Sindhi heart, would pour herself another helping of kadhi. But at the end of the day, both dishes were equally cherished in their kitchens—proof that while their flavours came from different worlds, the love for food and family was universal.

They may not have fully crossed the bridge of each other's culinary worlds, but they sure made a valiant attempt.

Sindhi Kadhi: A Tangy Hug in a Bowl

Oh, Sindhi kadhi. If there ever was a dish that could make your taste buds dance and your heart skip a beat, it's this one. It's the kind of comfort food you never knew you needed—spicy, tangy, and loaded with vegetables that are soft and perfectly soaked in all that gorgeous gravy. It's a riot of flavours and textures, and once you try it, you'll understand why it's loved by so many.

Let's dive right in and make this gem of a dish, shall we?

(Serves 4)

Ingredients

- 2 tbsp gram flour—this is the heart of the kadhi
- 1 tbsp oil
- 1 tsp cumin seeds
- 3–4 green chillies, chopped
- 1 tsp turmeric powder—we need that golden glow
- 1 tomato, chopped—because every dish deserves a juicy twist
- 250 gm okra
- 150 gm small brinjals
- 125 gm drumsticks
- 125 gm cluster beans
- 125 gm dudhi (bottle gourd)

(All vegetables have to be washed, cut into long slices, and left to marinate in salt. The cluster beans are left uncut, only trimmed.)

- 3–4 cups of water
- Red chilli powder (optional, if you'd like that extra fiery magic)
- 2 tbsp tamarind juice, for that tangy kick
- Salt, to taste for balancing all the goodness

- Fresh curry leaves
- Fresh coriander leaves—for garnish, of course

Method

1. In a hard-bottomed sipri, heat the oil.
2. Add the gram flour, keep the flame low. You don't want to burn it. Keep stirring until the oil and the flour unify. The aroma wafts through the house like the heavenly shower of blessings.
3. Add the cumin seeds and the chillies. Give everything a good stir.
4. Add 3 or 4 cups of water, stirring continuously to prevent lumps. Let it all come to a rolling boil.
5. Add turmeric and salt. You can add a teaspoon of red chilli powder for that extra fire.
6. Add the cluster beans first, they take longer to cook. Cover the pot and let it all simmer on low flame.
7. Next add the drumsticks, brinjal and the bottle gourd. Let this also simmer for 7–10 minutes.
8. Then add the okra. 5 to 7 minutes later, add the tomatoes.
9. Pour in the tamarind juice and bring the entire thing to a good boil. By now, the aroma has filled your senses and you are reminiscing about all the good times of your life.
10. Watch as the kadhi starts to thicken and turn into a luscious, aromatic delight. Throw in the curry leaves and top it off with fresh coriander leaves.

This delicious, tangy Sindhi kadhi is best served with steaming hot rice. And trust me, once you've had it with some crispy aloo tuk on the side, you'll never want to look at any other gravy the same way again.

Enjoy this tangy comfort hug in a bowl.

Aloo Tuk: The Crispy, Crunchy, Dreamy Potato Delight

Alright, folks, get ready to experience a potato dish that'll have you questioning every other potato recipe you've ever tried—aloo tuk. This little piece of crispy heaven is about to become your next obsession. It's crunchy on the outside, soft on the inside, and oh-so-flavourful. If you've ever been to a Sindhi wedding feast or a family gathering, you know aloo tuk is the life of the party. And if you haven't, well, buckle up for this flavour explosion.

(Serves 3)

Ingredients

- 4–5 medium-sized potatoes (because potatoes are everything)
- ½ tsp red chilli powder (let's spice things up)
- 1 tsp cumin powder (for that earthy warmth)
- 1 tsp coriander powder (adds that tangy kick)
- A pinch of turmeric
- ½ tsp aamchur powder—for that zing
- Salt, to taste (this is a must, no compromise here)
- Oil, for frying (it's fry time, baby)

Method

1. Start by peeling the potatoes and dicing them into big chunks. Wash them thoroughly, drain the water and let them marinate in salt.
2. Heat the oil in a deep-frying pan. When the oil is nicely hot, reduce the heat and gently

slide in the potatoes. Fry till you are sure they are soft to the core. Take care, they should not be so soft that they crumble.

3. Remove the fried potatoes from the pan onto a plate. Let them cool a bit. Now starts the flattening game. Take each potato, and press it down gently until they're about half their original thickness. Not too thin, not too thick. You want them to hold their shape but still get nice and crispy. Perfect.

4. Double it up. Heat the oil again and this time let the heat be high. Drop the flattened potatoes. Fry them until they're golden brown and super crispy on the outside. Think of that satisfying crunch when you take a bite.

5. Once they are crispy, remove and drain them on a paper towel. Transfer to a serving bowl. Now bring out the spice mix. Sprinkle the chilli powder, turmeric, cumin, and

coriander powder. Finally, sprinkle the aamchur. Give them a good toss.

6. Your aloo tuk is ready to be devoured. Serve them as an appetiser, side dish, or just as a snack while you're watching your favourite show (they're that addictive). The best part? You can pair it with green chutney, yoghurt, or even sweet tamarind chutney for that tangy-sweet contrast.

Pro Tip

Want to take it to the next level? Sprinkle a little more chilli powder and chaat masala right before serving to add that extra oomph.

There you have it—aloo tuk, the crispy potato delight that'll make your taste buds dance. Try it once, and I promise, you'll never look at potatoes the same way again.

Marching shoulder to shoulder with the kadhi is the sambar. How? See for yourself.

Kalyana Sambar: A Wedding in a Bowl

Let's set the scene: You walk into a South Indian wedding. There's the sound of the *nadaswaram* (the double reed wind instrument from South India) in the air, jasmine garlands everywhere, and the unmistakable aroma of THE sambar that can only mean one thing—*kalyana* sambar. But here's the best part: you don't need to crash a wedding to get a taste of this showstopper. This sambar brings the big, bold, and beautiful flavours of the feast right into your kitchen, no RSVP needed.

What makes this sambar legendary? Oh, it's the love, and that perfect balance of tangy, spicy, and downright soulful goodness. It's the kind of dish that'll have you shamelessly ladling it over your rice, again and again (and again).

And my Amma? She was the undisputed queen of kalyana sambar. Sure, you can follow the recipe, but let's be real: her touch was pure magic. When her sambar simmered away, it wasn't just food—it was a fragrant hug that filled every corner of the house and every heart in it.

Why is it special?

Because it's got everything—whispers of tradition, a pinch of nostalgia, and a whole lot of spice. This sambar doesn't just sit on your plate; it dances on your taste buds, and trust me, it'll have you hooked.

So, whether you're cooking it for your family of ten or two, one thing's for sure: you're about to recreate wedding vibes without the chaos. And who doesn't want a little extra spice in their life?

So, buckle up. Let's get our hands spicy and cook this wedding-worthy sambar, shall we?

(Serves 4)

Ingredients

For the Tempering

- 1 tbsp sesame oil—a generous dollop, don't be shy
- 1 tsp rai—because mustard is the life of the party
- ½ tsp fenugreek seeds—the unsung hero of sambar
- 1 tsp asafoetida

For the Sambar Powder (This Is Where the Drama Is)

- 1/2 tsp ghee
- 1 tbsp coriander seeds
- 1/2 tsp black peppercorns
- 1 tbsp tuvar dal
- 4 dried red chillies
- 1 tbsp chana dal
- 1/4 tsp fenugreek seeds

- 1 tsp cumin seeds
- 1 tbsp grated coconut

For the Sambar

- 1 cup tuvar dal (because no sambar is complete without it)
- A bowl of mixed vegetables, cleaned and chopped/sliced (okra, drumsticks, eggplants, yellow pumpkin, onions are usually avoided at weddings)—don't skimp, the more the merrier
- 2 cups of water
- Salt, to taste
- 1 cup tamarind water

- 1/2 tsp of turmeric powder
- A small cube of jaggery
- A few curry leaves and coriander leaves

Let's Get *Sambar-ing*

1. Rinse your tuvar dal and cook it in 3 cups of water in a pressure cooker until it's soft and mushy. You want it falling apart soft—none of that *al dente* stuff.
2. In a deep pan, heat the oil (oh yes, let the magic of tempering happen) and throw in the rai. Let them pop like tiny firecrackers. Add the fenugreek seeds and let the sizzling sound tell you it's working. Drop in some curry leaves for that waft of heaven. Add the asafoetida.
3. Add the onions (if you're using them), next add the okra and sauté till they shrink. Add all the other vegetables for that veggie goodness and sauté like you mean it.
4. Add water, turmeric, jaggery and salt, and let the veggies cook till they are tender.
5. Add the tamarind water for the tangy wink. Leave it to boil for 5 minutes.
6. Meanwhile, let's get the sambar powder underway. In a skillet, heat some ghee. Add coriander seeds, chana dal, tuvar dal, cumin seeds, peppercorns, red chillies, and fenugreek seeds; sauté till the colour changes.
7. Then add coconut and sauté till it turns aromatic and changes colour.
8. Turn off the stove and let it all cool down.
9. Transfer to the mixer and grind to a smooth powder. By now, your kitchen is bathed in the heavenly aroma.
10. Make a paste of the sambar powder by mixing a dash of water.
11. Add this to the veggies swimming in the tamarind water.
12. Bring it all to a gentle boil. And now, the magic of wedding sambar—drop in that cooked and mashed tuvar dal, and let everything come together.
13. Stir it gently and let it simmer for 10–15 minutes. The longer it simmers, the richer the flavour.

14. For your final touches, add in some chopped coriander leaves, and a drop of sesame oil. Once your sambar is at that *perfect*, velvety consistency, give it a taste. You should have a fine balance of tang, spice and a little sweet. Adjust the salt, consistency or jaggery as needed—you're the sambar maestro here.

Serve this kalyana sambar over a bed of piping hot rice, topped with a generous dollop of ghee (because we're all about that life). Or, pair it with a crispy vada or a soft idli and let the wedding feast begin. Or, if you want to do it like the pro-wedding hosts, pair it with some potato curry and there you have it—a wedding in a bowl.

Beans and the Bond of Flavours

Beans don't often find favour in my Sindhi household. It's not that we dislike them outright, but they rarely make us light up with anticipation—except when it's cluster beans. And not just any cluster beans, but the way Mamma made them, with her signature magic touch.

She stirred them into a symphony of flavours with a fragrant mix of garlic, fresh coriander, and tomatoes. The aroma of sizzling garlic and the tangy sweetness of tomatoes mingling with the slightly bitter bite of cluster beans—it's the kind of dish that leaves everyone scraping their plates clean.

But what made this dish even more special was Amma's love for it. Amma wasn't much of a beans-loving person either, but when Mamma made cluster beans her way, Amma always got the first and largest helping. Mamma would ladle out a generous portion and send it over with a gleam in her eye, as if sharing something precious.

In Amma's kitchen, cluster beans were an even rarer sight. On the occasions she did make them,

they took on a completely different form. Amma transformed them into an *usili*—a southern-style stir-fry enriched with paruppu (crumbled dal). This preparation was completely alien to the Sindhi palates, and honestly, they weren't fans. Yet, somehow, Mamma loved it. Maybe it was the effort Amma put into cooking it, or maybe it was the warmth of their shared food memories.

Isn't it strange how food carries stories and emotions? While cluster beans might not be a universally celebrated vegetable, in our family it became a bond between two kitchens, two hearts and two distinct culinary styles.

Another tradition that added to the charm of Mamma's cluster beans dish was the way she always paired it with sanna pakoras. Light, crisp, and delicately spiced, these fritters—explained in detail earlier in the book—added a delightful crunch to the meal. It was a pairing that turned a simple weekday lunch into a feast worth remembering.

So, while beans might not top the list of our favourites, this humble dish continues to hold a special place in our hearts and on our table. Because sometimes, it's not just about the taste—it's about the love that goes into it and the connections it fosters.

Amma went about the usili with nimble precision. The aroma of the steamed dal floated through the house like a soothing balm. The snappiness of the bean mingled with the crumbly dal took this creation to a celestial level.

Kothavarakkai Usili: Cluster Beans Stir-Fry with a Lentil Twist

(Serves 3)

Ingredients

For the Dal Magic

- ½ cup chana dal (so versatile)
- 2 dried red chillies (add some fiery fun)
- 1 tsp cumin seeds (the quiet flavour hero)
- A pinch of asafoetida (it's small but mighty)
- Salt, to taste

For the Stir-Fry Extravaganza

- 2 cups *kothavarakkai* (cluster beans), trimmed and chopped (yes, it's a labour of love)
- 2 tbsp oil (go for coconut or sesame oil—it's the South Indian way)
- ½ tsp rai (pop-pop goes the tempering)
- 1 sprig curry leaves (don't skip these—they're the soul of the dish)
- Salt, to taste

Method

1. Wash and soak the chana dal for 2 hours. Don't skip this step—it makes all the difference.
2. Drain the dal and toss it into a blender with red chillies, cumin seeds, asafoetida, and salt. Grind it into a coarse paste (no water, folks—let's keep it thick and crumbly).
3. Spread that dal paste onto a greased plate or idli mould like you're crafting a masterpiece. Steam it for 10–12 minutes until it's firm enough to crumble.

Pro Tip

Let it cool before you get handsy—no burnt fingers here.

4. Now, crumble it like a pro. Forks, hands—use what works for you.
5. Boil the cluster beans in salted water until they're tender but still a little snappy. Drain them and set aside.

6. To get the tempering started, heat some oil in a wide pan (because drama needs space). Add rai and wait for the pop—don't miss this little kitchen concert. Toss in the curry leaves and let them sizzle their way to aromatic bliss. In goes the crumbled dal—stir, sauté, and watch it turn golden and glorious.
7. Add the cooked cluster beans and mix everything like you're throwing a party in the pan. Adjust the salt if needed.
8. Cook for another 2–3 minutes, just enough to let the flavours mingle.
9. Pair this warm, nutty, crunchy delight with steamed rice and a drizzle of ghee. Trust me, it's comfort food at its quirkiest best.

Gwar Patata Sabzi: Cluster Beans with Potato

If you had told me back in the day that this humble cluster bean dish would steal the family spotlight, I'd have rolled my eyes. But Mamma's magic touch had a way of turning the most unassuming ingredients into household stars. Other Sindhi kitchens have their versions, sure, but for me? It's Mamma's way or no way. And yep, I've nailed it just like her—fresh coriander and all. It's now a fan favourite in my house too.

Here's the lowdown:

(Serves 3)

Ingredients

- 250 gm cluster beans, washed, trimmed, and cut into 1-inch pieces
- 1–2 potatoes, peeled, washed, and chopped into chunky 2-inch cubes
- 7–8 cloves of garlic (this makes all the difference)
- A small bunch of fresh coriander (the unsung hero of this recipe)
- 3 green chillies (or more, if you're feeling fiery)
- 2–3 tomatoes, ripe, juicy, and ready to shine
- Salt, turmeric, and coriander powder

Grind into a Paste

Blend the tomatoes, garlic, coriander, and green chillies into a glorious greenish-red paste that smells like pure heaven.

Method

1. Heat 2 tablespoon of oil in your trusty pressure cooker (where else would this magic happen?).
2. Drop in the paste and sauté until the oil decides to part ways with the sides. That aroma? Oh, it's a hug from Mamma herself.
3. Toss in the cluster beans. Give them a good swirl so they feel the love.
4. Enter the potatoes—mix 'em up well. (We're building friendships here, one veggie at a time.)
5. Sprinkle the salt, turmeric, and coriander powder like you're blessing the dish with good vibes. Mix it all till the veggies are happily coated.
6. Add half a cup of water and cook on medium flame. Remember, it's a dry dish, so we're keeping things minimal.
7. Seal the deal with the pressure cooker lid. Two whistles later, the magic's done.

Pro Tip

Serve it piping hot with soft phulkas for that extra crunch.

And oh, don't forget the sanna pakoras on the side. This pairing? Chef's kiss.

So, what are you waiting for? Get cooking and let Mamma's legacy live on.

The Rasam–Vada Affair Amma, Mamma and a Bowl of Bliss

This book of fond food memories would be incomplete without a twist in the tale of the two kitchens. The star of the show? The queen of Tamil cuisine—the rasam.

It's the story of rasam from Amma's kitchen and vada from Mamma's hands. Who doesn't love rasam in all its glory? Be it tangy tomato, zesty lemon, or fiery pepper—it's a hug in a bowl.

Mamma was absolutely mad about rasam, especially Amma's version. She drank it like soup—cup after cup. But the real magic happened when she made vadas to go with it. Rasam-Vada was her thing.

Picture this: Amma's hearty, soul-soothing rasam paired with Mamma's golden, crispy vadas. She'd let those fluffy dumplings swim in the rasam, then carry a bowl to her room, switch on her favourite soap opera, and savour every spoonful with a blissful smile.

Mamma wasn't one for behind-the-scenes culinary drama, especially the kind Amma tried so passionately to dish out. While Amma waxed poetic about her eeya chombu for making rasam—a gleaming, sacred tin vessel that could've been part of a treasure hunt for all we knew, Mamma stayed blissfully unmoved. 'It's just a pot, right?' she'd

mumble under her breath, much to Amma's horror.

Amma's lectures on rasam-making were a full production in themselves. She'd point to the simmering liquid with the authority of a Michelin-star chef, delivering her golden rule: 'The rasam must never boil like it's angry at the world. Just a gentle foam on top—that's where the magic lies.' Mamma? Oh, she'd nod along, her face the picture of politeness, but her eyes? Firmly fixed on the steaming bowl of rasam, calculating how long it would take to claim it from Amma's hands.

And then there was the finale, the *pièce de résistance*: the delicate scattering of finely chopped coriander on top of the frothy rasam. Amma treated this moment like a royal coronation, explaining the significance of 'sealing the flavour'. Mamma? She didn't care about any coronation. She cared about one thing: 'When can I eat?'

If Amma's rasam-making was an art form, Mamma's philosophy was simple: Skip the drama, serve the rasam. And honestly? Both approaches worked like a charm.

Sadly, a couple of years ago, Amma's sharp memory began to falter, and with it, her once-unshakable confidence in the kitchen began to waver. One day, in a moment of forgetfulness, she left her beloved eeya chombu on the gas stove. Now, anyone familiar with the eeya chombu knows its Achilles' heel: it heats up quickly and can melt into a silvery pulp if left unattended. And yet, in 50 long years, Amma had never made this mistake—not once.

That day, however, her prized possession—her pride, her constant companion in crafting the perfect rasam—melted away into an unrecognisable blob. It wasn't just a pot that was lost. For Amma, it felt like a part of her identity, her legacy in the kitchen, had slipped away with it.

Watching her grapple with that loss was heartbreaking—a reminder of how the simplest objects can carry the weight of cherished memories, of traditions lovingly passed down, and of the pride we find in the everyday magic we create.

Though the eeya chombu was gone, her rasam and the love she poured into every pot would always stay with us. And now, when the aroma of rasam wafts through our home, it's like Amma from across the lobby is gently reminding us that her essence is far bigger than a vessel—it's in the stories, the flavours, and the love she gives us every single day.

Tomato Rasam: Food Therapy at Its Best

(Serves 3)

Ingredients

- 2 ripe tomatoes (the stars of the show)
- 1 cup thin tamarind extract (sour and sassy)
- ½ tsp turmeric powder
- 1 tsp black peppercorns (the secret weapon)
- 1 tsp cumin seeds (the co-conspirator)
- 1 slit green chilli
- ½ inch ginger
- 1 dried red chilli
- 2 pinches of asafoetida for the zing
- Salt, to taste
- 2 tbsp cooked tuvar dal (for that creamy comfort)
- 1½ cups water
- A few curry leaves (aromatic and authentic)
- A few coriander leaves (a fresh finish)
- ½ tsp rai
- 1 tsp ghee (liquid gold)

Method

1. Mix tamarind extract, chopped tomatoes salt, turmeric, asafoetida, slit green chilli, ginger, and dried red chilli in a pot. Add water, bring to a boil for 10 minutes on medium flame.
2. Add the mashed tuvar dal and add more water. Let it all froth (don't boil).
3. Grind the black peppercorns and cumin seeds in a mixer. Leave the powder coarse. Now add this flavour bomb to the frothing rasam. Stir once—underplay your emotions. Keep the flame on low. Garnish with chopped coriander.

4. Switch off the stove when you have a nice layer of froth.
5. In a skillet, heat the ghee. Add the rai and watch it splutter. Switch off the stove and add the curry leaves. Pour this tempering lovingly over the frothy rasam.
6. Serve with hot rice and any veggie curry (or just drink it straight up like Mamma used to do).

There you go—a rasam that's quick, soulful, and utterly unforgettable, just like Amma and Mamma's bond.

The Legacy of Two Kitchens

As I look back on the many dishes, the laughter, the little moments of miscommunication and the joy of shared meals, I realise something profound. The recipes in this book are more than just a collection of ingredients and steps; they are the story of two mothers—from different cultural backgrounds—who, through their love for food, brought their worlds together in the most magical way.

Amma brought the traditional Tamilian grace and a love for the simple, soulful flavours of the south. Mamma, on the other hand brought her spirited Sindhi boldness, always ready to spice things up. These two remarkable women, each with their own way of living, of nurturing, and of loving; showed us that food is never just about what's on the plate—it's about what it brings to the table.

They didn't just teach us how to cook. They taught us how to connect, how to bridge divides and how to savour life's little contradictions. They showed us that when two kitchens, two cultures, two hearts meet, the result is a harmony of flavours, a feast of stories and a banquet of love. Whether it was the sweet bitterness of the pavakkai pitlai, the soothing warmth of kadhi, or the delightful crunch of a fried aloo tuk—each dish was a reminder that food is the universal language of home.

As their daughter, I have taken their precious recipes, and woven them into the fabric of my own kitchen. In every dish I prepare, I blend their

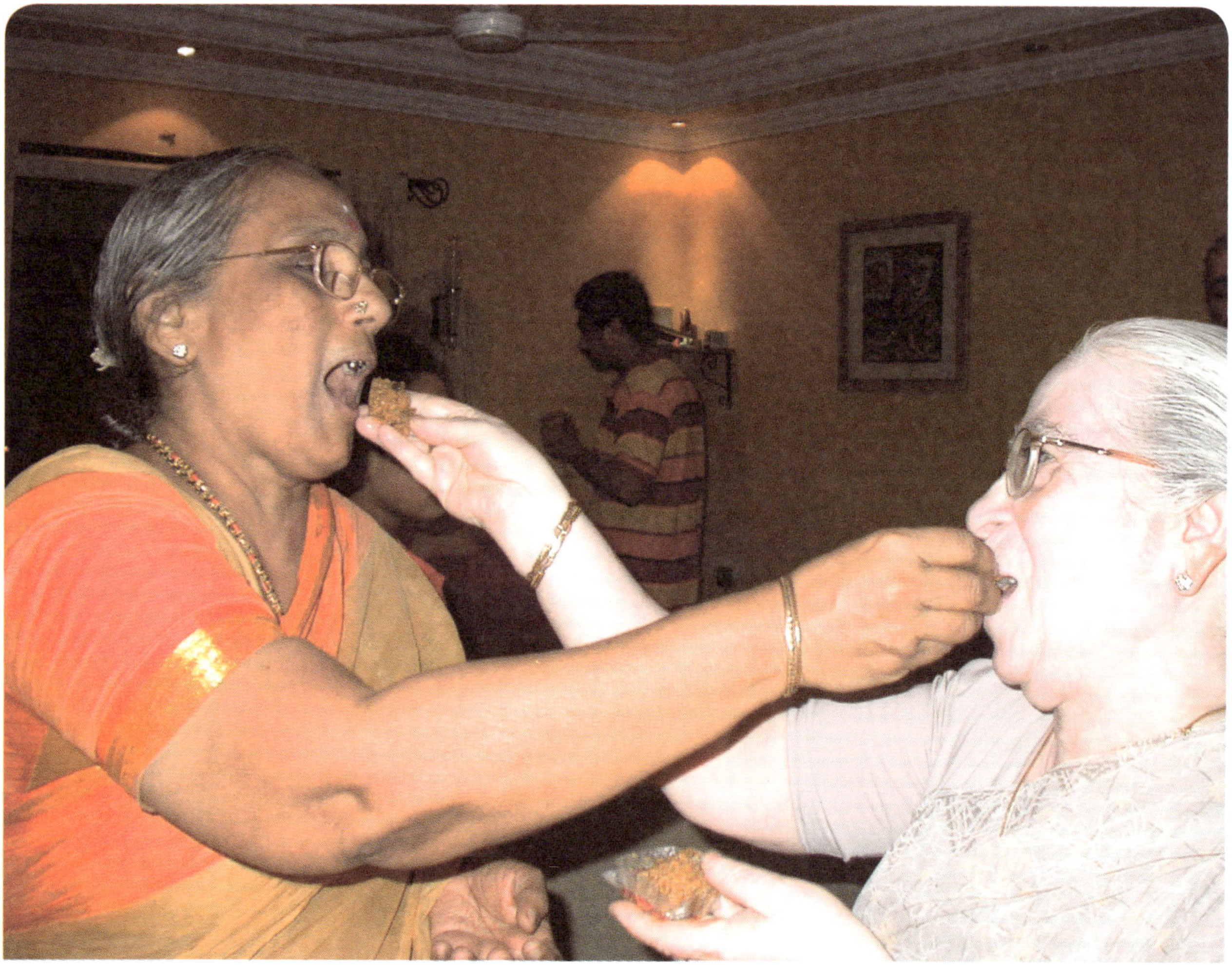

flavours, their techniques, and their love; creating new memories while honouring the old. The aroma of Amma's rasam and Mamma's gwar patata mix in my kitchen, just as their voices once filled the air, telling stories, sharing laughter, and passing down wisdom. These recipes are no longer just their legacy—they are now mine, and in them, their spirit lives on.

So, as you try your hand at these recipes, know that you're not just cooking a dish—you're carrying forward a legacy. A legacy of two mothers who, through the alchemy of their kitchens, created something far greater than the sum of their ingredients. A legacy of love, laughter, and the shared joy of breaking bread together. And with each meal, you're creating your own everlasting memories.

As we sit down to enjoy the meals that they so lovingly prepared for us, we celebrate not just the food, but the bonds that tie us—across cultures, across generations, and across kitchens. Here, we celebrate two special women.

To Amma. To Mamma. To the food that brought them together, to the memories that live in every bite, and to the love that still binds us.

Bon appétit!

Acknowledgements

They say too many cooks spoil the broth. This book proves otherwise. It simmered, spiced, and sparkled because everyone stirred the pot with love.

What began as a personal journey in the kitchens of my two mothers, turned into a feast of shared laughter, long phone calls, frantic photo shoots, taste tests, nostalgic tears, and a whole lot of joy. These pages carry food memories, yes. But also, the sweet memories of making memories.

This book carries not just recipes but memories, nostalgia, loving hands, soothing voices, camera clicks, WhatsApp nags, emotional meltdowns, and heartfelt belly laughs. It's a *thali* of life, and here's everyone who helped plate it:

Lalitha, the listener of laments, dispenser of hugs, cheerleader-in-chief, and my literary agent from the Gods. From the time First Forays took me under its wings, you've been there, reminding me who I am when I forget. I owe you filter kaapi and a lifetime of thanks.

Nikhil, you turned memory into magic. Your photos didn't just capture food—they captured emotion, history, and the very steam of nostalgia. You've given these dishes a second life, and I am forever grateful.

Anitha, the brilliant illustrator who brought soul to the margins—your sketches add that warm, whimsical touch that words alone couldn't capture. Every line of your art is a story in itself. That we pulled this off over nothing but patchy WhatsApp calls, you being in the US, me in India, is nothing short of a miracle. And yet, you got it. You saw the book exactly the way I felt it. Thank you for making the margins sing.

A huge, heartfelt thank you to **Bidisha** and the fabulous team at **Amaryllis Publishing**—for believing in this story, for letting it breathe, and for turning it into a book I can hold, gift, and cherish. Thank you, **Trisha**, for treating every chapter with care, every comma with love, and every page with purpose. It's been an absolute joy to work with you all.

To my family and friends—thank you for reminiscing the past with me, for saying, 'Remember when…' and for helping me bottle fond memories in the pages that now forever hold them. You brought the flavour, the feeling, and the food.

Kaush, the newest tadka in my family. Thank you for being my photo shoot warrior, my sounding board, and for bringing the sparkling girl energy in our boy-heavy world. Your ideas are like perfectly puffed pooris—light, golden, and always welcome. Thank you for lifting, laughing, and lighting up every room you walked into during this journey.

Sagar, my son, my fiercest critic. My proudest achievement. You blew hot and cold on this project, and I wouldn't have it any other way. You questioned, challenged, rolled your eyes, and in doing so, made this book sharper, better, truer. Your voice is in every line, even when silent. You are the chilli, the salt, and the secret ingredient all rolled into one. And the fact that you know it? Even better.

Sunil, dear husband, anchor, partner-in-crime through not just this book, but five! Through every late-night edit, every 'I hate this chapter' rant, every false start and fragile finish—you stood steady. You've been the signpost when I lost my way, the gentle nudge when I froze, the wind beneath my rather stubborn wings. I couldn't have done any of it without you.

And finally, to the two mothers who shaped our kitchens, our lives, and our souls. You taught me that meals are more than food—they are memory, love, and a quiet legacy. This book is dedicated to you.